THE CULT

OF OUR LADY OF GUADALUPE

★ ★ ★ THE

CULT OF OUR LADY

★ ★ ★ ★ ★ ★ ★ OF

GUADALUPE

★ ★

A HISTORICAL STUDY

By
SISTER
SIMONE
WATSON, O.S.B.

THE LITURGICAL PRESS   COLLEGEVILLE, MINNESOTA

THE CULT OF OUR LADY OF GUADALUPE – A HISTORICAL STUDY by Sister Simone Watson, O.S.B., was originally submitted to the Faculty of St. John's University in partial fulfillment of the requirements for the degree of Master of Arts of Sacred Science.

Photo credits: Mr. John Dominik, front cover; Mr. Luke Judd, pp. 33, 34; Mr. Alfonso Marcué, pp. 35, 36; Mr. Merle Wachter, pp. 37, 38, 39, 40, 41, 42, 43; Mr. Alexander Von Wuthenau, p. 44.

Nihil obstat: Paschal R. Botz, O.S.B., S.T.D., *Censor deputatus. Imprimatur:* ✠ Peter W. Bartholome, D.D., Bishop of St. Cloud. August 10, 1964.
Printed and bound by the North Central Publishing Company, St. Paul, Minnesota.

FOREWORD

It is a pleasure to write a foreword to Sister Simone's scholarly paper on the cult of Our Lady of Guadalupe. From acquaintance with all that has been published in English since Our Lady of Guadalupe began to be known in the United States (around the turn of this century), it is clear that this modest work meets a real need.

Sister Simone gathers together in brief compass the full convincing evidence both for the genuine historical character of the Guadalupan events and for the devotion consequent upon these facts as recognized and directed by ecclesiastical authority.

In our day the relatively late origin of the existing manuscript accounts of the apparitions evokes question of their validity. Spanish and native sources unavailable in English are here presented to show that the general story of the apparitions is supported and verified by many other documents of profane history, either contemporary or at least of the same century.

There are the *mapas* or picture chronicles of the Aztecs, together with manuscript histories made by them once they had learned to set their own language in script. Then there are the religious ballads or *cantares*, more or less contemporary, bearing on Guadalupe, and various references to it in wills or testaments of the period, and in secular histories and diaries of varied origin; several of these diaries are in English.

To these one must add the weight of the unbroken oral tradition of the Mexican people and their great devotion to Our Lady of Guadalupe from the beginning. The Mexican hierarchy is witness to this by its unwavering attitude of protection and encouragement of the Guadalupan cult.

Requisite confirmation by the Holy See is indisputable. In the sixteenth and seventeenth centuries we have the granting of indulgences by various Popes, encouraging the devotion. In the eighteenth century Benedict XIV approved a special Mass and Office of Our Lady of Guadalupe and made her the National Patroness of Mexico. In the nine-

5

teenth century Leo XIII ordered the sacred Image to be crowned in his name, which was done in 1895. In our own century Pius XII, in 1945, renewed this coronation. His words are pregnant with meaning. "We are certain," he said, "that so long as you (Our Lady of Guadalupe) are recognized as Queen and Mother, America and Mexico will have been saved."

This papal confirmation is backed by the tradition of miracles flowing from Our Lady of Guadalupe. Above all is her gift to America: the loving "living miracle" of the glorious Image itself, most beautiful in its simplicity, perduring over centuries, speaking with silent eloquence her message of maternal mercy to all.

This wealth of accumulated information assures us that we are on firm ground in our devotion, and our hearts are warmed so that the final section of theological reflections on the Guadalupan message becomes particularly impressive. Our Lady comes at Tepeyac as Mother of God and Mother of men, bringing grace and promise of comfort and relief in every need.

The reader would do well to begin with the appendix. It contains Coley Taylor's delightful version of the Spanish of Luis Lazo de la Vega's chronicle, redolent with the sweet fragrance of Our Lady of Guadalupe herself, Mother of all America and of the world. May she lead us to Jesus her Son!

Feast of Our Lady's Assumption
August 15, 1964

✠ Fr. M. Columban Hawkins, O.C.S.O.
Abbey of Our Lady of Guadalupe
Lafayette, Oregon

CONTENTS

INTRODUCTION

On the ninth of December, 1531, ten years after the conquest of Mexico, the Most Holy Mother of God appeared to Juan Diego, an Indian neophyte, on the rocky slope of Tepeyac. She came as a native princess; she asked that a church be built there. With tender words of compassion and love, she declared herself to be the merciful Mother of men:

> Deeply and intensely do I desire that a temple be raised here. Here I shall show, manifest, and give all my love, my compassion, my help, and my protection to mankind. I am your merciful mother; yours, and all those who live united in this land; and of all other peoples who are my loving ones, who cry to me, who seek me, and who trust in me. Here I shall listen to their weeping and sadness in order to remedy and alleviate their many sorrows, needs, and miseries.[1]

Four times she spoke with the Indian, and on the twelfth of December she confirmed the truth of her visitation. On the *tilma*[2] of Juan Diego which had carried roses to the Bishop of Mexico,[3] Fray Juan de Zumárraga, there miraculously flowered the beautiful Image that has since been venerated under the title of Our Lady of Guadalupe. In the moment that Fray Juan de Zumárraga fell upon his knees before the Holy Image, the first seed of the Guadalupan cult was sown. Deeply rooted in tradition and history, it has grown into a mighty tree whose branches now extend into many lands.

No greater proof of the miraculous nature of the Image of Our Lady of Guadalupe exists than the testimony of the constant devotion with

[1] Angel M. Garibay, "La Maternidad Espiritual de María en el Mensaje Guadalupano," *La Maternidad Espiritual de María*, Conferencias leídas en los Congresos Mariológicos, 7–12 octubre 1957 y 9–12 octubre 1960 (México: Editorial Jus, 1961), p. 194.

[2] A cloak made of maguey or palm fibre used by the Aztec Indians. Also known as an *ayate*.

[3] Juan de Zumárraga arrived in Mexico as Bishop-elect in 1528. In 1533 he was consecrated in Spain. Antonio Pompa y Pompa (ed.)., *Album del IV Centenario* (México: Basílica de Santa María de Guadalupe, 1938), p. 27.

9

which it has ever been honored. More than four centuries of unequalled veneration testify that this Image is of divine origin. Those who lovingly venerate the Virgin of Tepeyac firmly believe in the genuineness of the apparition. They "know" that Our Lady of Guadalupe is their mother; they confide in her loving message; they rest safe "in the fold of her mantle, in the cross of her arms for protection." [4]

It is not to prove the authenticity of the apparition of the Virgin of Tepeyac that this work was undertaken. The principal concern of this study is to present the analytical documentation of the Guadalupan history, the objective investigation of the miracles worked through Our Lady's intercession, and the approbation of the Holy See upon which belief in the cult of the Virgin of Guadalupe is based. In the same way that this researched body of facts is essential for a valid belief in the cult, it is likewise the starting principle for the intrinsic theological implications contained in Our Lady's heavenly message. A brief treatment of the theology of the Guadalupan message, therefore, will conclude this historical study.

The scope of documentation which supports the cult of the holy Virgin of Guadalupe is broad. Sources dating back to the sixteenth century and continuing to the present time offer a colorful and varied field of investigation. These documents range from fragments of primitive records to scholarly commentaries and historical investigations. The variety of sources makes even more unique the invariable truth which never fails to emerge from this manifold body of facts.

The celestial Image itself is the most eloquent document. For over four hundred years it has silently enlightened and indoctrinated the faithful, and has been the fruitful inspiration for historical study and research. This synthesis of the documentary evidence of the apparition finds its principle in this heavenly Image, the source of light, that will draw this same body of evidence into the radius of its divine Center.

[4] Garibay, p. 201.

★

PART ONE

★

★

HISTORICAL DOCUMENTATION

FOUNDATION OF THE CULT

★ CHAPTER ONE

ANCIENT INDIAN SOURCES

No official document of the sixteenth century verifies the Guadalupan apparition as no primitive ecclesiastical record substantiates the prodigy of 1531. Undeniable testimonials, however, make the principal facts associated with the tradition of the apparition morally and historically certain. The Fathers of the Fifth Mexican Provincial Council in 1896 considered this unbroken chain of tradition so reliable that they did not hesitate to urge the faithful to venerate as authentic the apparition of Our Lady of Guadalupe:

> For although the portentous apparition is not a mystery or dogma of faith, it should, nevertheless, be admitted and respected as believed since ancient times; it is worthy of credence for it is supported by uninterrupted tradition and by irrefragable testimonials.[1]

The most primitive sources which help establish the historicity of the event are Aztec documents. It was on an Indian *tilma* that Our Lady left her holy portrait, and it is to this chosen race that we owe the first evidence of the miracle. So memorable an event naturally caused a deep and lasting impression on the Mexican Indians. It was their singular privilege and, as such, was preserved with great fidelity. The story of the heavenly visitation was first transmitted by word of mouth and then conserved with great precision in their historical records.

Guadalupan writers are in agreement that the most primitive data recorded by the Indians are found in their *mapas* or picture-chronicles. These maps were used by the natives to illustrate some outstanding happening which they wished to keep for posterity. In this system of hieroglyphics, small figures of men, birds, beasts, fish, and plants were painted on a type of brown paper or goatskin which had been treated until it had the appearance of white parchment. These picture-chronicles were guarded by the priests and are as authentic as any modern his-

---

[1] *Quinto Concilio Provincial Mexicano: 1896* (México: Imprenta El Catecismo, 1900), p. 124. This and all following citations from Spanish sources have been translated from the original by the writer.

torian's record.[2] The composition of these ancient symbolic drawings was never left to mere fancy or to the imagination of those executing them:

> The one entrusted with the making of these *mapas* did not represent his imaginings and whims, but portrayed with figures well known the events whose memory he wished to conserve. . . . He was rigorously limited to depict all with an exactitude that was as precise as it was expressive. . . . For this reason only wise men who were well versed in history and well capable of artistically portraying it could make these *mapas*.[3]

Among the picture-chronicles which have survived the ravages of time, a small number have been found which contain clear and precise allusions to the apparition of Our Lady of Guadalupe. Exacting historians regard them as valuable documents of authentic information.

Luis Becerra Tanco, Oratorian priest, linguist, and scholar of the seventeenth century, testifies to the existence of a map compiled before the conquest of Mexico. In his book, *La Felicidad de México*, he certifies that he saw and read

> . . . a map of notable antiquity written in the ancient figures and characters of the natives which recorded the happenings of more than three hundred years before the coming of the Spaniards to this kingdom and then for many years afterwards; . . . and among the events which occurred after the pacification of this city and the kingdom of Mexico there was figured the miraculous apparition of Our Lady and her blessed Image of Guadalupe.[4]

Lorenzo Boturini Benaducci, a Milanese gentleman, is responsible for much precious Indian documentation. Arriving in Mexico in 1736, he conceived the idea of writing a documented history of Our Lady of Guadalupe. He spent long years and great sums of money forming his valuable collection. An imprudent attempt to have the Picture solemnly crowned resulted in a clash with the government of Spain. He was deported and many of his manuscripts were lost. Some fragments of maps and parchments were finally brought to the National Museum of History in Mexico where they can be seen today.

Among his valuable manuscripts we find reference to the following picture-chronicle:

> A map of cotton cloth, as large as a sheet, where in various quarters the general conquest is drawn . . . and what most charms me is the

[2] Luis Becerra Tanco, *La Felicidad de México* (México, 1685), p. 25.

[3] Fortino Hipólito Vera, *Contestación Histórico Crítico en la Defensa de la Maravillosa Aparición de la Santísima Virgen de Guadalupe* (Querétaro, México: Imprenta de la Escuela de Artes, 1892), p. 456.

[4] Becerra Tanco, p. 29.

Image of Our Lady and Patroness of Guadalupe with the first hermitage in the background.[5]

Don Lorenzo Aztatzontli, an Indian of Cuautitlan,[6] painted a chronicle in which he described in Aztec symbols the apparition of Our Lady.[7] At the judiciary process of 1666, his daughter Juana de la Concepción swore that her father, who was very dedicated to the making of maps, had made one of the apparition. She ended her testimony by saying that her father had told her what was written on the map about the miracle, and that he had heard all of it from Juan Diego himself.[8]

Other *mapas* and codices which show detailed illustrations of Our Lady form a varied and interesting collection of data. The above cited examples are sufficient, however, to demonstrate the antiquity and authenticity of this medium of transmitting the tradition.

The second method employed by the Indians to conserve the memory of some great event was that of "singing" the story. These ballad-like songs were called *cantares*. They were composed by the priests in a certain proper meter and taught to the children who, when they became adults, sang them in dances called *mitotes*. Father Francisco de Florencia, Jesuit historian of the eighteenth century, writes that before the great flood of 1629, the Indians gathered in the plaza dressed in the rich plumage of birds called *quetzatotome*.[9] They formed a large circle and danced to the tune that two old men made on an instrument called the *teponaztli*, while they sang, in a meter peculiar to the Nahuatl or Aztec language, the story of the apparition.[10]

The members of the First Provincial Council, held in Mexico in 1555, were so fearful that the newly converted Indians might return to their idolatry that they prohibited "songs of ancient rites and histories, unless said songs were first examined by religious or persons who well understood their tongue."[11] Thirty years later the Third Council reinforced the order that all historical songs must be examined by the clergy and that "a month before singing them they must be brought before the bishop for examination and approval."[12]

---

[5] Lorenzo Boturini, *Idea de Una Historia General de la América Septentrional* (Madrid: Imprenta de Juan Zúñiga, 1746), p. 152.

[6] Juan Diego's birthplace, which lies eighteen miles northeast of Mexico City.

[7] Francisco de Florencia, *La Estrella del Norte de México* (México: Doña María de Benavides, 1688), p. 54.

[8] Archivos de la Basílica de Santa María de Guadalupe, *Información de 1666* (Manuscript copy of original, October 27, 1751), p. 31.

[9] Bird similar to bird of paradise.

[10] Florencia, p. 95.

[11] Francisco Antonio Lorenzana (ed.), *Concilios Provinciales: 1ero. y 2ndo: 1555–1556* (México, 1769), p. 146.

[12] Mariano Galván Rivera (ed.), *Concilio III Provincial de México: 1585* (México: Eugenio Maillefert y Co., 1859), p. 321.

Reliable witnesses certify that the *cantares* of the apparition were publicly sung in the presence of the archbishop and clergy.[13] The subject matter of the songs, therefore, must have been acceptable and in accord with the decrees of the councils. For years the Indians sang the story of Our Lady, and they were never silenced by the ecclesiastical authorities, who were extremely severe in regard to the singing of *cantares*.

On December 26, 1531, fifteen days after the apparition, the Holy Image was taken from the main church to the small adobe hermitage which the Indians had constructed. As the procession advanced, the miracle was proclaimed by a song accompanied by a drum. This song is known as the *Pregón del Atabal* [Proclamation to the Drumbeat]. Is this a Guadalupan hymn? Father Mariano Cuevas, S.J., who found the document among some sixteenth-century manuscripts, sees the fourth verse of the *pregón* as very determinate. The synthesis of the miracle of Tepeyac is clear:

> Yehuan Dios Mitzyocox aya xochitla ya Mitztlacatc yancuicatl mitzcuiloa Santa María in Obispoyac.[14]

> God created the Most Holy Mary
> In the midst of most miraculous flowers
> And He has renewed thee again
> In the Bishop's painting.[15]

The name Guadalupe is not used in the song. At first the Indians referred to Our Lady as *Tonantzin,* who later became *Nuestra Madre,* "our mother." Ten years after the apparition, the title of Guadalupe was common to all. The fact that the name is not mentioned confirms the antiquity of the document:

> The contemporary original of this valuable, typical Mexican *cantar* is not known; perhaps it was not even written at the time it was sung; it was perpetuated by ear among those who listened to the Mexican bard who transmitted the loveliest of our traditions to the sound of the drum. In order that these songs would not be lost with time and forgotten, a friar and his disciples, so it seems, dedicated themselves to collect these *cantares* in the last third of the sixteenth century.[16]

Aztec chronicles comprise the third source of primitive documentation. These annals were written by Indian scribes who, after they had

---

[13] Cayetano Cabrera y Quintero, *Escudo de Armas de México* (México, 1746), p. 323.

[14] Mariano Cuevas, S.J., *Album Histórico del IV Centenario Guadalupano* (México: Basílica de Santa María de Guadalupe, 1931), p. 22.

[15] Donald Demarest and Coley Taylor, *The Dark Virgin* (New York: Coley Taylor, Inc., 1956), p. 202.

[16] Cuevas, p. 23.

been taught to write the Nahuatl language, interpreted the *mapas* in writing.

In Boturini's *Catálogo Indiano*, a descriptive listing of his collected manuscripts which is found in the *Idea de Una Historia General de la América Septentrional*, mention is made of a valuable Indian record.

> . . . a Nahuatl manuscript. It treats of many things pertaining to the Mexican empire, and in a few lines, written in concise style, reference is made to the apparition of the Holy Lady on the hill of Tepeyac. The author did not put the correct Arabic numbers of the year in which the apparition took place but the account is ancient, worthy of belief.[17]

It is not surprising that the dates of the Mexican annals do not always coincide with the common calendar. The annalists were Indian and their knowledge of the Spanish system of numbering was very limited. They — and of course the Spaniards also — frequently confused the Arabic numbers with the Mexican chronological symbols. Hence there is no absolute concordance between the dates of the Mexican calendar and the common one. "In regard to the precision of dates, thirty or forty years after the Conquest, the Indians were absolutely lost; and, therefore, they are no authority in chronological dates."[18]

According to Don Wigberto Jiménez Moreno, an outstanding Mexican archaeologist and anthropologist, the Mexicans of that era had no less than five different calendrical systems which varied widely.[19]

An interesting example of this in reference to Our Lady of Guadalupe is found in the *Anales de México y sus Contornos* [Annals of Mexico and Its Surroundings]. There we read, "1556 — XII *Pedernal*[20] The Lady descended to Tepeyac; in the same year the star smoked."[21]

The date given for the apparition is twenty-four years later than historically believed. The clue, however, to 1531 being the exact year of the coming of Mary to Tepeyac is found in the second clause, "the same year the star smoked."

> The year 1531 is established beyond question in all records Indian and Spanish. An interesting detail provided by some of the Indian annals is the notation that "Our Lady of Guadalupe appeared in the year of the 'smoking star.'" . . . I learned that the "smoking star" was unquestionably Halley's Comet. In all accounts of the history of this comet, 1531 is given as one of the years of its spectacular

[17] Boturini, p. 85.

[18] Cuevas, p. 48.

[19] From unpublished lectures on Meso-American Chronicles, Spring 1963, Castillo de Chapultepec, México.

[20] System of Mexican chronology.

[21] Primo Feliciano Velázquez, *La Aparición de Santa María de Guadalupe* (México: Imprenta Patricio Sanz, 1931), p. 65.

brilliance, and a key year in helping the English astronomer for whom it is named to establish its periodicity by enabling him to trace it back as far as 1066. The Aztec interest and achievements in astronomy would make this a matter of importance to the Indian chroniclers. . . .[22]

Father Augustino de la Rosa in his scholarly work, *Dissertatio Historico Theologica de Apparitione B.M.V. de Guadalupe*, written in 1887, refers to a book of annals which twice mentions the apparition. "Praedictum versionem ipse vidi, atque etiam textus mexicanus B.M.V. Apparitionem testantes."[23] The Nahuatl entry found in these annals refers to the vision seen by Juan Diego.

> acaxiuiti 1531 — otlalmanque in caxtilteca in cuitlaxcoapa ciudad de los angeles in Juan Diego oquimo tenextilli in tlazo cihuapilli de Guadalupe Mexico motocayotia Tepeyacac.[24]

It is believed that this is the same comprehensive annal which was deciphered in 1790 by Doctor Bartolache. He found the manuscript in the Library of the Royal University and describes it as a "notebook in manuscript with twenty-five pages which had in the margin diverse figures painted with an ink pen."[25] The 1531 and the 1548 entries are translated:

> In the year of the three *cañas* [the figure is that of a reed and the number thirteen is below=1531] the Spaniards took possession of Ciutlaxcuapa, City of the Angels, and Juan Diego received the vision of the loved Lady of Guadalupe called Tepeyac.

> In the year *pedernal* [year of the flint which coincides with 1548] died Juan Diego to whom appeared the loved Lady of Guadalupe.[26]

Extant copies of sixteenth-century testaments mention in a general way the apparition and the Image as facts well known and established. These wills comprise the last source of primitive evidence to be treated. One such document used by Boturini to prove the antiquity of the cult, *"ad probandum antiquum Dei parae cultum,"*[27] was the last will of Don Francisco Verdugo Quetzalmamatictzin. In this legacy of 1563, the testator explicitly requests that a sum of money be taken to the church of Our Lady of Guadalupe:

---

[22] Coley Taylor, "The Anti-Apparitionists," *Mexico Quarterly Review*, Vol. I, No. 3 (Fall 1962), p. 185.

[23] Guadalaxarae, 1887, p. 98.

[24] *Ibid.*, p. 99.

[25] José Bartolache, *Manifiesto Satisfactorio* (México: Imprenta por Felipe de Zúñiga, 1790), p. 37.

[26] *Ibid.*, p. 69.

[27] Boturini, *Catálogo Indiano*, p. 5.

Mando que si Dios me llevare de esta vida, luego se lleven cuatro pesos de limosnas a Nuestra Señora de Guadalupe para que me las diga de Misas el Sacerdote que reside en dicha iglesia.[28]

In a sermon preached on the fourteenth of December, 1777, Father Joseph Fernández de Uribe supported the antiquity of the Guadalupan cult by using as evidence a will written by an Indian on March 11, 1559.[29] A copy of another similarly dated testament exists and can be seen today in the National Museum of Archeology, History, and Ethnography in Mexico. The original was written on paper of the maguey plant which was used long before and immediately after the conquest. In this testimonial the testator leaves three pieces of land to Our Lady of Guadalupe, ". . . for my very much loved Lady Holy Mary of Guadalupe who appeared on Saturday."[30]

Due to the grammatical translation of the Nahuatl, the name of the bequeather is not clear. The existence of several similar wills dated exactly the same but bearing different names has caused historians no small confusion. Some believe that two distinct wills were written by different Indians of Cuautitlan on the same day; others claim the existence of only one document in which the name has become confused. For the purposes of this study it is sufficient to know that testaments do exist and substantiate the fact that only twenty-eight years after the miraculous visit of Mary, her cult was firmly established.

The non-existence of contemporary official records is lamented. This lack, which might present a problem in the demonstration of the solid basis upon which devotion to Our Lady of Guadalupe is founded, serves rather to emphasize the truly marvelous manner in which Providence has preserved the truth of the miracle. The testimonies of the Indian sources testify unquestionably to the authenticity of the apparition of the Blessed Virgin to Juan Diego in the year 1531. These primitive and irrefragable documents form the first link in the unbroken chain of tradition.

[28] *Ibid.* (English text) I ask that if God take me from this life, four pesos of alms be taken to Our Lady of Guadalupe so that the priest who resides in the church may use them to say Masses for me.

[29] Joseph P. Fernández de Uribe, *Sermón de Nuestra Señora de Guadalupe: Predicado en su Santuario El Año de 1777 Día 14 de Diciembre* (México: Oficina de Mariano de Zúñiga, 1801), p. 18.

[30] Biblioteca del Museo Nacional de Arqueología, Historia, y Etnografía, México, MSS, 156.

★ CHAPTER TWO

HISTORICAL NARRATIVES

The latent significance of the Tepeyac message which lies hidden in crude Indian recordings takes on clarifying tones in the written narratives of the sixteenth century. There are more than twenty indisputable references to Our Lady of Guadalupe in this century which help make understandable the heavenly message and establish the historicity of the event.[1]

There is one document of signal importance which does give an undeniable basis for the moral certainty of the apparition and for the authenticity of the message. The author of this contemporary manuscript, which is known as the *Nican Mopohua*,[2] is still a matter of controversy. The majority of reliable critics, however, agree that the writer was the scholarly Aztec, Don Antonio Valeriano, who is believed to have written between the years 1530 and 1540. He was one of the first students of the Franciscan *Colegio de Santa Cruz de Tlatilolco*[3] founded by Fray Juan de Zumárraga. It is thought that he was one of the four scribes who collaborated with Bernardo de Sahagún, Franciscan historian, in the editing of ancient manuscripts. The Nahuatl scholar, Monsignor Angel M. Garibay, is of the opinion that Valeriano was only a co-author of the Guadalupan account. This he deduces from the diversity of style in which it is written:

> . . . Antonio Valeriano, who was a resident of Azcapotzalco, his place of birth, and who was so capable in his thought and activities that he governed the Indian community of Mexico for a period of thirty-five years. He was born in 1524 and died in 1606. The excellence and superiority of this Indian, married to a descendant of Moctezuma, has caused the glory of the Guadalupan manuscript to be attributed to him. He was a co-author, but not a sole author.[4]

[1] Garibay, p. 189.
[2] The first two Nahuatl words which begin the account. It is now the common practice to designate the work by this title.
[3] Variant spellings for the same Mexican proper names are found in the original documents. All variants are correct.
[4] Garibay, p. 193.

19

Boturini, however, affirms the sole authorship of Valeriano. His *Catálogo Indiano* contains a reference to some fragments of an historic manuscript which he attests were copied from the original by the famous Mexican historian, Don Carlos Sigüenza y Góngora. To Boturini it is evident "that Don Antonio Valeriano, native of Atzcapotzalco, a noble Indian and a teacher of rhetoric at the imperial *Colegio de Tlatilulco*, wrote the history of the apparition of Guadalupe in the Nahuatl tongue."[5]

Whether Valeriano is the author or co-author, it is to him that the title of "Evangelist of the Apparitions of Tepeyac" is given. This classic work, the *Nican Mopohua*,[6] is of major importance because it is the source of all later accounts. The original document has been lost. After the death of the author in 1606, it passed into the hands of Don Fernando de Alva Ixtlilxochitl, a descendant of the Texcoco kings, a lover of knowledge and holiness.[7] Luis Becerra Tanco verifies the fact that de Alva did possess the Valeriano papers at one time:

> He had in his possession a notebook written, in letters of our alphabet in the Mexican tongue, by an Indian of the *Colegio de Santa Cruz* . . . in which the four apparitions of the Holy Virgin to Juan Diego are found.[8]

From Fernando de Alva the manuscript passed into the hands of Don Carlos de Sigüenza y Góngora, who testified in 1668 that "I found this account among the papers of Don Fernando de Alva and I have all of them. The original is in the writing of Don Antonio Valeriano, Indian and true author."[9] On the death of Sigüenza, he willed the manuscript to the Jesuit *Colegio de San Pedro y San Pablo*, from where it was transferred to the Royal University of Mexico. In 1847, during the war between the United States and Mexico, all of Sigüenza's documents were taken from the archives where they were guarded, and carried away by the victors. The fate of this precious manuscript remains enveloped in deep mystery even until today. Father Enrique Torroella, S.J., cites Alfonso Junco, Catholic Mexican scholar, as believing in the probable existence of the original *Nican Mopohua*:

> The original which belonged to Sigüenza until now has been lost with a great number of valuable documents collected by that scholar during his exemplary life. These he willed to the *Colegio de*

[5] Boturini, *Catálogo Indiano*, p. 86.
[6] José M. Beristáin de Souza, *Biblioteca Hispano-Americana Septentrional* (México: Oficina de Alejandro Valdés, 1821), III, 252.
[7] Becerra Tanco, p. 30.
[8] *Ibid.*
[9] Fernández de Uribe, *Disertación Histórico-Crítico* (México: Oficina de D. Mariano de Zúñiga, 1801), p. 82.

San Pedro y San Pablo; they were later passed on to the University, left the country secretly and perhaps can now be found in the United States or Europe.[10]

Two copies of the original are now conserved in the Public Library in New York City and form part of the manuscript collection, *Monumentos Guadalupanos.*

The narratives based on this first chronicle are many and varied. Yet all the histories, sermons, and poems repeat in different ways the substance of the Valeriano story. The variations which occur are of little note; the essential truth is always present:

> It is the exclusive property of truth never to vary; and the Guadalupan history, no matter in what form it is presented, will always be the same — in the sixteenth, the seventeenth, the eighteenth, the nineteenth centuries and always.[11]

Nothing was publicly printed about the apparition of Tepeyac until Father Miguel Sánchez gave his Spanish account to the press in 1648. Since he could not find any manuscripts, he searched among primitive records. "I had recourse to the curiosity of the ancients which I found among some authentic writings."[12] These he used without leaving any reference to the documents consulted; he was content to state that he had used ancient sources. As a mystic and exegete, his treatment is more of a panegyric of the miracle than an historical work.[13] He follows the narrative faithfully, but he is constantly reading mystical meanings into it. One is reminded of Saint Augustine, for whom Father Sánchez had great admiration. Juan Diego and the Bishop, Juan de Zumárraga, are the generous Jonathan and the modest David: "Let Juan Diego represent the generous Jonathan; the Bishop, modest David, shepherd of the flock of Mexico."[14] The Virgin Mary is seen as Bride and as City: "As Bride, since she is the true Bride of God; and as City since she was herself representing her own city of Mexico."[15] This Biblical interpretation was the first public appearance of the Guadalupan story. The charm and poetry of this document did not, however, affect the cult as much as a 1649 transcription in Nahuatl of the Valeriano account.

This seventeenth-century work, *Hvei Tlamahuicoltica,* published by

[10] Enrique Torroella, S.J., (ed.), *El Nican Mopohua* (México: Buena Prensa, 1961), p. v.

[11] Vera, p. 448.

[12] Anon., *Santa María de Guadalupe* (Guadalajara, México: Tip. de Ancira Y Hno., 1884), p. 257.

[13] Fernández de Uribe, *Disertación* . . . , p. 70.

[14] Miguel Sánchez, *Imagen de la Virgen María de Guadalupe* (México: Imprenta por la Viuda de Calderón, 1648), pp. 48–49.

[15] *Ibid.*, pp. 29–30.

Luis Lazo de la Vega, is considered one of the most vital contributions to the history of the apparition.[16] Although Luis Lazo de la Vega, chaplain at the Hermitage of Our Lady, printed the Nahuatl work as his own, it is now universally accepted that it is but a transcription of the Valeriano papers. This is understandable since the rights of authorship were not considered at that time.

A sixteenth-century copy of the original *Nican Mopohua* was found among Boturini's manuscripts. This account passed with Boturini's treasures to the Library of the Royal University. It was seen there by an anonymous author who wrote a description of it. He affirms that the account is incomplete, but that it accords perfectly with the Lazo de la Vega narrative. Referring to this anonymous description, Alfonso Junco writes the following in an article printed in the newspaper *El Universal* on February 17, 1931:

> An unedited document exists in the Library of New York City [José Fernández Ramírez Collection]. It is an anonymous manuscript. According to the paper the author was an erudite man and lived at the end of the eighteenth century. He states that he saw in the Royal University among Boturini's manuscripts the account of the apparition on an ancient paper [metl — from the maguey plant]. It goes only as far as the end of the third apparition, but it is identical to the Luis Lasso account.[17]

Boturini himself verifies his ownership of the *Hvei Tlamahuicoltica*. He says that this cannot be an original work, but should be attributed to Valeriano.[18] The contribution made by Lazo de la Vega to the fund of historical Guadalupan documents remains, nevertheless, of great consequence. Through his faithful transcription, the prime sources of all future narratives were to be given to the public.

The last of the three chronicles which consolidated the firm foundation of the cult of Our Lady of Guadalupe is another seventeenth-century contribution made by Father Luis Becerra Tanco. In an answer to a request made by the Apostolic Commission, Father Becerra Tanco put the Nahuatl story into Castilian. He had read the original manuscript when it was in the possession of Fernando de Alva.[19] His lucid rendition of the Tepeyac story was used in the Apostolic Process of 1666. It was first published under the title *Origen Milagrosa del Santuario de Nuestra Señora de Guadalupe* and was later known as *La Felicidad de México*.

---

[16] The English translation, which was rendered from the Spanish text as found in the *Album de la Coronación de la Santísima Virgen de Guadalupe* (México, 1895), is taken from *The Dark Virgin*. See the Appendix to this work.

[17] Jesús García Gutiérrez, S.J., *Primer Siglo Guadalupano: Documentación Indígena y Espanola* (México: Imprenta Patricio Sanz, 1931), p. 65.

[18] Boturini, *Catálogo Indiano*, p. 80.

[19] García Gutiérrez, p. 62.

Becerra Tanco was a man of great talent and he was exceptionally well prepared to write this great work. He had at his command the best tradition and the best manuscripts as well as a thorough knowledge of Indian customs, traditions, and language. He was educated at the Royal University, where he later became professor of science and literature.[20] "Many fruitful labors are recorded of him; but as things now appear, his greatest work was his elucidation and authentication of the Guadalupan history."[21]

To the authorized testimonies of Valeriano, Sánchez, Lazo de la Vega, and Becerra Tanco, the cult of Our Lady in Mexico is indebted for its final clarification. These four evangelists of the "good-tidings" of Tepeyac brought Our Lady's message out of obscurity into the effulgence of day.

The opinion that nothing at all was written about the apparition until the mid-seventeenth century, however, is false. Already in the second half of the sixteenth century, direct references were made in several secular histories to the sacred Image and to the cult as something well known and accepted. Thirty-seven years after the miracle, Bernal Díaz del Castillo, a contemporary witness and a highly acceptable historian, mentions Guadalupe with great certitude. This rough soldier-companion of Cortés refers to the Shrine of Our Lady of Guadalupe on two different occasions.

> Look at the Holy House of Our Lady of Guadalupe which is on Tepeaquilla,[22] where the camp of Gonzalo de Sandoval was when we won Mexico; and see the holy miracles which it has worked and works each day. And let us give many thanks to God and to his blessed Mother Our Lady for it.[23]

When speaking of Cortés sending one of his men to Tepeyac, he adds, "to the place which is now called Our Lady of Guadalupe where are wrought and have been wrought many miracles."[24]

This unbiased and incidental mention of the miraculous Shrine is very conclusive, especially when it is recalled that in 1568 the writer had been away from Mexico for many years, even though he had been there at the time of the apparition and for seven years following.[25]

Around the same time that this contemporary New World historian

[20] Velázquez, p. 104.

[21] George Lee, C.S.Sp., *Our Lady of Guadalupe* (New York: Catholic Publishing Company, 1946), p. 128.

[22] The name given by the Spaniards to the hill of the apparition in order to differentiate between it and another hill named Tepeyac.

[23] Bernal Díaz del Castillo, *Historia Verdadera de la Conquista de la Nueva España* (Spain, 1837), p. 250.

[24] *Ibid.*, p. 189.

[25] Lee, p. 126.

was writing, Don Juan Suárez de Peralta was finishing his great work, *Tratado del Descubrimiento de las Indias*. This Indian historian, who had once been the mayor of Cuautitlan, gives undeniable evidence of the great devotion of the faithful to the Virgin of Guadalupe in the mid-sixteenth century. The texts cited demonstrate to what extent the cult had grown in a few decades. For although Suárez de Peralta finished his manuscript in Seville in 1589, he recounts the happenings of many years previous.[26] Speaking of the arrival of the Spanish viceroys to Mexico, he gives testimony that they always visited the Shrine of Our Lady before taking possession:

> At each village where he [Augustín de Villanueva] arrived he was received with great honor, as it is customary to do for all viceroys who come to our land, and thus he arrived at Our Lady of Guadalupe, which is about two leagues from Mexico, a picture of great devotion which has worked many miracles [it appeared among some crags and all the land has recourse to this devotion].[27]

The next significant reference to Our Lady is found in the works of the Franciscan friar, Bernardo de Sahagún. Besides spreading the Word of God, he also contributed to the culture of New Spain by his historical works. When treating of the sacrifices and the idolatry which were formerly offered on Tepeyac, he mentions the fervent devotion of the natives to Our Lady and reprimands the misuse of her name. The Indians were accustomed to offer solemn sacrifices to their goddess *Tonantzin*[28] on the hill of the apparition. After Our Blessed Lady revealed herself to them as their mother, they continued to call her by the pagan name. Sahagún criticizes this manner of addressing the Mother of God. "It is something that should be remedied because the proper name for the Mother of God and Our Lady is not *Tonantzin* but *God-Nantzin* or *Teonantzin*."[29]

From these contemporary historical passages cited by men of sound judgment and truth, it is evident that in the very century of her appearance Our Lady of Guadalupe was already an object of veneration and love.

An interesting and unique testimony is recorded by the Renaissance historian and anthologist, Richard Hakluyt. In October of 1568, Sir

---

[26] Cuevas, p. 81.

[27] Juan Suárez de Peralta, *Tratado del Descubrimiento de las Indias* (Madrid: Imp. de Manuel Hernández, 1878), p. 161.

[28] "Our Mother." She was supposed to have given birth to *Teohuitznáhuac* without violence to her virginity. She was invoked as an advocate for rain. Jesús Amaya, *La Madre de Dios: Génesis e Historia de Nuestra Señora de Guadalupe* (México: Editorial Lumen, 1931), p. 223.

[29] Bernardo de Sahagún, *Historia de las Cosas de Nueva España* (México: Editorial Porrua, 1956), III, 321.

John Hawkins left some of his companions abandoned on the coast of the Gulf of Mexico. One of them, Miles Philips, wrote a diary of his adventures. It is the first time that the name of Our Lady of Guadalupe is mentioned in English. This report of an impartial observer who was an enemy of the Spanish as well as a non-Catholic is very significant.[30] The following entry is found among Philips' notes:

> The next morning we departed from thence on our journey to Mexico and so travelled until we came within two leagues of it where there was built by the Spaniards a very fair church called Our Lady's Church. . . . Whensoever any Spaniards pass by this church, although they be on horseback, they will alight and come into the church and kneel before the image and pray to Our Lady to defend them from all evil; so whether he be a horseman or a footman he will not pass by, but first go into the church and pray as aforesaid, which if they do not they think they shall never prosper: which Image they call in the Spanish tongue Nuestra Señora de Guadalupe.[31]

In the ancient *Anales de Juan Bautista*,[32] the arrival of the English captives to Mexico is authenticated.

> 28 octubre 1568 años — auh huollothui viernes yguac acico ynimalhuan visorrey yningleses tlaca 16.
>
> [28th of October 1568 — Friday dawned; then there arrived sixteen Englishmen prisoners of the viceroy.] [33]

The conclusive stone in this mosaic of historical chronicles is the poem written by Captain Angel Betancourt, a soldier who came to New Spain in 1608. This poem can be read in manuscript form in Volume I of the series of manuscript volumes of Mexican historical events which is now kept in the National Archives of Mexico City.[34] Verse forty-five contains a clear allusion to the supernatural origin of the Image. Father García Gutiérrez classifies these verses as of utmost importance:

> In them, expressed for the first time in Spanish, one finds the idea that God Himself painted the Virgin of Guadalupe on Juan Diego's mantle. No one could say that they show the influence of Miguel Sánchez, since his book was published many years after these

[30] Demarest and Taylor, p. 217.

[31] Richard Hakluyt, *The Principal Navigations, Traffiques, and Discoveries of the English Nations* (New York: Dutton, 1926), VI, 314–15.

[32] Biblioteca del Museo Nacional de Arqueología, Historia, y Etnografía, Colección Gómez Orozco, MS, 14.

[33] Velázquez, p. 10.

[34] Archivo Nacional de México, *Colección de Memorias de Nueva España*, Vol. I, 1790, p. 244.

verses were written — nor that these lines influenced him since they
were never published.[35]

The free translation of Betancourt's poem as found in *The Dark Virgin*
is, as the editors describe it, "more inspired than coherent, and more
valuable as history than as literature:"[36]

> My own Image of Guadalupe
> Not as Greeks were wont to limn
> Of common canvas, paint and clay
> My God, the True Praxiteles
> Will of His Art Myself portray.[37]

By the end of the seventeenth century, she who had appeared on the
shores of Lake Texcoco was reigning from the heights of her throne in
the Aztec capital. Many years were to pass before her title of Queen
of Mexico was to be officially proclaimed; but already, less than two
centuries after her apparition, her sway over the hearts of her subjects
was without rival. Unlettered Indians, historians, priests, scholars, and
poets had served her by safeguarding the memory of her heavenly
visitation. To this retinue, whose contributions have been considered in
the first part of this paper, the story of the miracle of Tepeyac owes its
initial preservation.

[35] García Gutiérrez, p. 120.
[36] Demarest and Taylor, p. 205.
[37] *Ibid.*

PART TWO

TRADITION AND MIRACLES

THE PRINCIPAL SUPPORTS OF THE

GUADALUPAN CULT

★ ★ CHAPTER THREE ★

THE WITNESS OF TRADITION

The most expressive testimony of faith that can be given to an object of veneration is the constant, devout, and reverential homage with which it is honored.[1] This continuous faith in the reality of the apparition has great historical significance. For more than four centuries, a persistent and universal cult has ever given great integrity to the Guadalupan tradition. Already in the mid-eighteenth century, a solid and general cult flourished:

> Even though more than two hundred years had gone by since the first prodigious Apparition . . . one could not enter into palaces, religious cloisters, private homes, or poor hovels without his eyes being delighted at once by lovely copies of the marvelous Image.[2]

Since comparatively little had been written up to this time about the miracle of 1531, on what was the extraordinary growth of the Guadalupan cult based? Father Antícoli, the great Jesuit defender of the authenticity of the devotion, roots the flowering cult of Our Lady in a solid and legitimate tradition. Even though there have been few documents to assure the faithful, posterity received the knowledge of the singular favors which the Mother of God deigned to perform for the Mexicans from the living local voice which handed down this account.[3]

Tradition is accepted in philosophy as one of the four criteria of truth. It bears so much import in theology that His Holiness Benedict XIV stated and established as a general rule that witnesses who have seen and heard have the same authority and demonstrative power as historical documents.[4] This oral tradition is one of the principal foundations upon which the Catholic faith is based:

[1] Fernández de Uribe, *Disertación* . . . , p. 56.
[2] Francisco Lazcano, *La Maravillosa Aparición de Santa María de Guadalupe* (México: Impresa Rafael Cadena, 1853), p. 342.
[3] Esteban Antícoli, S.J., *Defensa de la Aparición de la Virgen María en el Tepeyac* (Puebla, México: Imprenta del Colegio Pío de Artes y Oficios, 1893), p. 55.
[4] Benedict XIV, *De Servorum Dei Beatificatione et Beatorum Canonizatione* (Patavii: Typis Seminarii, 1743), III, 50.

It is the infallible argument of many articles of our faith; the Fathers and Doctors of the Church have used this mighty arm to defeat heretics; it is the bulwark of human faith and history; it is the channel whereby mankind has learned of antiquity.[5]

Real tradition must have certain qualities which distinguish it from mere hearsay. It must be immemorial and common and general to all classes of people, invariable and uninterrupted.[6] The tradition that surrounds the miracle of Tepeyac has all these qualities to authenticate it. It is immemorial since, from the very year of the apparition, the Image became the object of an enthusiastic devotion. As has been pointed out previously, a representative cross-section of all classes and people embraced Our Lady as their common Mother and Queen. In spite of the fact that the history of the apparition was written by Indians and Spaniards in an era of discord and was diffused by the traditions of many peoples, the details are always found to be constant and exact.[7]

With reference to Our Lady of Guadalupe, invariability is the most conclusive proof among the four characteristics of tradition. It is notable that the details of the story have been recorded with such exactitude in spite of the crude methods of transmission. The number of apparitions, the names, the messages, the dates — all are without exception the same.

Rich and varied stones form the pillar of Guadalupan tradition. Long chapters would be needed to treat such an extensive topic of a history that is exceedingly broad. For this history is not only an account of a miraculous Image; it is the story of a nation and of a people whose whole destiny was forged by the apparition of the Mother of God. A definitive treatment of the miracle would be necessary in order to show how it is interwoven with secular history, conflicts, triumphs, and failures. Since such a comprehensive study is not within the scope of this work, only one notable event in the line of tradition will be considered.

The Apostolic Process which was held in Mexico City in 1666 convincingly illustrates the power of the living voice to conserve the truth of tradition. For many years it had been the wish of both the clergy and the faithful to keep December 12th as a day of precept with a proper Mass and Office. This desire was finally formulated in a request to His Holiness Alexander VII in 1663. The tradition of the miracle was signed by 137 of the most illustrious Catholics of that time. It was accompanied by the episcopal decree in which the Bishop [8] authorita-

[5] Fernández de Uribe, *Disertación* . . . , p. 56.
[6] *Ibid.*, p. 43.
[7] *Ibid.*, p. 46.
[8] His Excellency Diego Osorio Escobar y Llamas, Bishop of Puebla. In Mexico City there was a *Sede Vacante*. Velázquez, p. 195.

tively affirmed the truth of the apparitions and the faithful devotion of the Mexican people.[9]

The answer to the petition was received in the form of an order from the Congregation of Rites to begin a plenary and formal investigation of the apparition. This rescript contained the questions to be used by the judges in the examination of the witnesses of the miracle and the circumstances surrounding it. In the year 1666, the Canonical Chapter ordered the judiciary process to be opened. Theologians, canonists, historians, scientists, painters, and doctors gathered together on January 7 for the solemn opening which began the judicial investigation. In these proceedings "the constant tradition of the Mexican Church of the miracle was proved authentically and juridically." [10]

Since the Process was 135 years after the apparition, it was impossible to examine eye-witnesses. The testimony of those who had not seen but heard about the happening was examined since the juridical value of such witnesses is of equal force. Twenty such ear-witnesses were examined:

> If the causes are ancient, it is necessary to use as proof not the testimony of eye-witnesses who can no longer possibly exist, but that of ear-witnesses.[11]

The first witnesses who under solemn oath testified in favor of the apparition were a group of aged Indians from Cuautitlan. From their grandparents and relatives, contemporaries of Juan Diego, they had learned of the marvelous event. Although some of those who were summoned were over one hundred years of age, they were still mentally keen and persons of great integrity.

Marcos Pacheco, aged eighty, was the first witness questioned. He had heard his aunt exhort him to virtue by these words:

> God make you like Juan Diego, native of this town where you too come from, whom I knew and treated familiarly, as also María Lucía [his wife] and his uncle Juan Bernardino. And Juan Diego was so good that the Most Holy Virgin appeared to him one Saturday in the morning as he was going to Tlatelulco.[12]

Pablo Juárez, governor of Cuautitlan, learned the story from his grandmother, Justina Cananea, aged 110. She had helped make the bricks for the hermitage and had been a close friend of Juan Diego. She knew the whole story. "It was so public and well known how it had all occurred that even the little children sang it." [13]

[9] Vera, *El Tesoro Guadalupano* (Amecameca, México, 1889), pp. 90–108.
[10] Antícoli, p. 38.
[11] Benedict XIV, III, 51.
[12] *Informaciónes de 1666 (Manuscript Copy . . .)*, p. 31.
[13] *Ibid.*, p. 75.

The oldest witness was Andrés Juan, who was 115 years old. He testified that

> . . . his father had taken him and many other Indians of this town to the blessed hermitage . . . and in this hermitage was the Image of Our Lady of Guadalupe on the *ayate* in the same form and manner as it remains today on the altar of the new hermitage which all the natives of this pueblo helped for weeks to build.[14]

He said that he was sure that Our Lady had spared his life so that he could honor her by his testimony.

The other five Mexicans who were examined likewise gave direct and clear testimonies. This evidence left no doubt regarding the solidity of the tradition among the Indians.

The second session of the inquiry took place in Mexico City where a number of clergy and religious were examined. Weighty contributions were made by Luis Becerra Tanco and Miguel Sánchez.

Becerra Tanco, whose account of the miracle was included in the final official report of the proceedings, testified the following:

> I affirm and bear witness that I have heard from persons entirely worthy of faith and credence and well known in this city of Mexico, respectable ancients who speak and understand the Mexican tongue with an elegant perfection themselves: who, speaking soberly, report the tradition as it has been set forth, certifying to have heard it from those who personally had known the natives to whom the Most Holy Virgin appeared, and also the most illustrious lord, Fray Juan de Zumárraga.[15]

He then gives the detailed testimonies of friends and relatives of Juan Diego, his uncle Juan Bernardino, and Fray Juan de Zumárraga.

Miguel Sánchez swore that he had heard the tradition of the apparition for fifty-three years. He said that when he had been gathering ancient sources for his book, he had interviewed the vicar of the hermitage. From him he learned that the reason for not finding any original documents was that there had been a great scarcity of paper and that the archives had been robbed.[16] Father Sánchez also testified concerning the tradition of Zumárraga's immediate response to so marvelous a favor. He said that the Bishop kept the Image in his oratory, where a great concourse of people gathered. He then took it to the main church, from which it was later taken to the hermitage in a solemn procession

> . . . in which the Secular and Ecclesiastical Chapters of the City took part . . . and this procession according to true and certain

[14] *Ibid.*, p. 26.   [15] *Ibid.*, pp. 117–18.   [16] *Ibid.*, pp. 55–57.

information was the twenty-sixth of the month of December of the same year 1531, fifteen days after the apparition.[17]

Many other valuable contributions were made by the numerous remaining witnesses. Once the evidence of this tradition was firmly established, interest and investigation were then ready to be directed to the Image itself which always remained the center of this tradition:

> Painters expert in art, famous doctors, and other qualified persons were authorized to conduct the juridical investigation made of the Holy Image. It was taken from the sanctuary and plainly placed in the presbytery where it was examined at length and minutely.[18]

After a detailed study of the picture according to the rules of art, the commission of artists reported that it was humanly impossible for any artist to paint something so perfect on such coarse and unprepared material, and that no artist was able to copy its color and perfection nor ascertain the medium used in the painting. They unanimously affirmed that "the Holy Image of Our Lady of Guadalupe imprinted on the *ayate* or *tilma* of said Juan Diego should be attributed to and understood to be a supernatural work and a secret reserved to the Divine Majesty." [19]

The report of the Physicians Royal of Mexico, Dr. Don Lucas de Cárdenas, Dr. Don Gerónimo Ortíz, and Dr. Juan de Melgarejo, concluded the proceedings. These eminent specialists all agreed that the damp and salty air which arose from Lake Texcoco, which lay near the site of the hermitage, was not a "natural help in preserving it . . . it should have caused its total ruin . . . and the fineness of its colors should have been dulled by the action of the nitrate." [20]

On April 14, 1666, the results of the judiciary process together with the traditional account of the apparition written by Becerra Tanco were sent to Alexander VII. Accompanying the documents was a letter written by the Secular Chapter:

> The City of Mexico, metropolis of the Kingdom of New Spain, prostrate at the feet of Your Holiness, confidently trusts to receive your Paternal Benediction, together with the favor it desires for the greater glory of the Divine Majesty to whom it owes the singular blessing of having been given the Image of the Holy Virgin, Mary, Mother of God, who appeared miraculously on the cloak of a neophyte.[21]

[17] *Ibid.*, p. 58.   [19] *Ibid.*, p. 108.   [21] *Ibid.*, p. 146.
[18] *Ibid.*, pp. 138–39.   [20] *Ibid.*, p. 140.

The church at Cuautitlan, Juan Diego's birthplace. Statue of Juan Diego wearing the *tilma* in the foreground.

"The Speaking Eagle," symbol of Juan Diego, whose Aztec name was Cuauhtlatohuac, "He Who Talks Like an Eagle."

Eugenio Cardinal Tisserant seated before the Image at the main altar of the Basilica of Our Lady of Guadalupe (August, 1964).

Admiring the crown from the coronation of 1895 are (left to right):
Mr. Alfonso Marcué; Rt. Rev. Guillermo Schulenburg, Abbot of the
Basilica of Our Lady; Eugenio Cardinal Tisserant; His Excellency
Miguel D. Miranda, Archbishop of Mexico.

Chapel located at the site where, according to one tradition, Juan Bernardino taught before the time of the apparition.

The Sanctuary of the Fifth Apparition, where our Lady cured Juan
Bernardino and announced her title of Guadalupe.

Maguey plants, from which the material of the *ayate* is made.

Mexican *charros* approaching the Basilica of Our Lady of Guadalupe through the main *Plaza de las Américas*.

Santiago de Tlatelolco, the Franciscan church to which Juan Diego was going on the morning of the apparition.

Charros on horseback approaching the entrance to the *Plaza de las Américas*. The Hill of Tepeyac, *El Cerrito*, is seen in the distance.

Indian dancers honor Our Lady of Guadalupe. The church at the left stands on the site of the original hermitage of 1531.

The main altar of the Basilica of Our Lady of Guadalupe.

Close-up of the Image

Close-up of the altar of the Basilica of Our Lady of Guadalupe.

Pages 46, 47, 48:

Copy of a sixteenth-century last testament. Taken from *Album Histórico Guadalupano del IV Centenario* by Mariano Cuevas, S.J. Manuscript in the New York Public Library.

Nican Mopohua. Taken from the manuscript collection *Monumentos Guadalupanos* in the New York City Public Library.

Prégon del Atabal. Taken from *Album Histórico Guadalupano del IV Centenario* by Mariano Cuevas, S.J. Manuscript in the National Library of Mexico.

Jesus. Mᵃ. y Joseph.

Nº 47

ica initocatzin Dios tetatzin, Dios tepiltzin, Dios Espiritu Santo yei
Persona ihuan in zan huel centetzintli Dios ticuih ihueli.

Axcan sabado a 11 de Marzo 1759 años inimachiotia iteh nitlato
a in nochan, Quauhtitlan oneh mocahuilili in notatzin
in nonantzin Maria martina ca huel nican notlacahan in iteahatzi

Cate

San Buena Ventura quauhtitlan no tlapilacal san Joseph huilo
inno huelnihuatzin Doña ines
thuatzin ieomo miquizque
inamictzin luisa Maria tteicauhtzin Gregorio macenyeo momina
innotlacatoga,
lique zan no cel oneo cauh innotlaco tatzin, mochin nomomi
ienopilhuan, ce omocauh notelpoh itoca francisco
nemi, anozo amo, intla nemir intla onicesoqui ic ilhuan ceme
vauh quicuizque, ceme ixtlamati tisoqui, mocalisoqui, ipan
tlatozque min amat tla cuitla, iquitlator no tlato
in notlal _____ ihuan inquenin niquiza in nican ipan altepe
Quauhtitlan ihuan tlapilacali San Joseph huillan in nican omo
huagauhtzino ra telpohtli Juan Diegotzin, quin tepan omo
namictizinoa in ompa Santa Cruz tlacpac inahuac San
Pedro. quimo namuin in ihpohtli itoca Magdalintzin, ic
ica omomiquili in ihpohtli, ca icel omo cauh in Juan
Diego _____ zakpan _____ inipaltzinco omocni
uh itlamahuitzoli in ompa tepeiacac:
nexpi in tlaco Cihuapili Santa Maria: in oncan
tlatzo _____ Guadalupe, ca huel nican toaxcatzin io
an to altepe Quauhtitlan aleuin in axcan huel nocia
ca cahuel _____ ca ti ne cotia, in notlaxcauilis nio
ne macnla _____ axca

46

Ni Can mo pohua moteε pa na in que nin
yan cui Can hue y tla mahui Col ti Ca mo nex i
ti in Cenquiz ca ich poch tli santa maria Dioz
y nantzin toh Ci hua pillatoh Catzin in on Can
te pe ya Cac mo... hue Cua ξa tzi yoc
A Cachtopa que moti titzin no Ce ma Cehual
tzintli i to Ca Juan Diego aca Ca te pan mau
xi ti ni tlaCo y xip tlatzin y nix pan yanzuic
obizpo Don fra g Juan de ξu mar ra ga yhuan
nix quich tlamah hue Colli ye que mo chi hui ti a
... mahtlac xi huitl in no pe hu tlo Catl
ye... mexi... Coin y e o mo man in mexi
Cu mallimye no... an on tlamatca
... Caniz tepeh huah... Can in me
Ca Canyeo peuh yexoitla ye tuepo ni tntzuncli
que ixtitzin nixi macho Catzin ni pal ne no juan
notteot Dioz In huel ih quac in panixhuitl
mili quini entoz y ue in ta yu no que huet
que yqui huivoc in me tztli Diziembre moch
on Cat Ca ξema Ce hual tzin ti te no tlah palten
... ti Ca Caxi Ca Juan Die go, ixhui i oc
on pa chane Cat Ca in quauh ti tla
Auh i ni Ca teoyotl oc mo chi om

Teponazcuicatl, o sea Cantar
al són del atabal.
Biblioteca Nacional de México. Sección de
manuscritos. "Cantares en Mexicano" Fol 27 r°.
2ª mitad y Fol 27 v° 1ª mitad
M. Cuevas S.J.

Tico toco toco tiquitiquiti quiti quito. Canic mocueptiuh.

Xilapapal xochicentli niyolaya nepapā tonaca xochitl moyahuaya
incueponti moquetzaco yanaya aya yeteoya ixpan tonaa
Santa Maria ay yo.

Ahuaya yacuicaya çanquehal axihuitl tomoli hui yanaya yenilā
cuial yceliztli y ye dios aya ni yhayotl aoya yehecoya
onca Hacuilohpā nemca moyollo amoxpehual ypan toncuicaya
tiquimonyaithua teteuctin aya in obispo ya çacatotahin aya
oncā tithatoa altitempā ay yo.

ye Juan Dios mihyocox aya xochtla yamitzthacatili yancuicatl
mihcuiloa Santa Maria in obispo yaoc

ohuicaihcuilihuia abaayada onthahoc amoxtli ya moyollo ya onaya
mocton ahuichuac oo tohecayotla ycaya ninemih yenilā ay yao

Acyanec hauili ac yenohuan ohual onicali a anni iteuhuan ay yan
cuicanitl yyehua y no xochiuh no cuica y huitequi onteixpā ay yo.

Hueyntlahc nicheqpin tomahicac quahuitl nic ycuiloa ya cuicatl yteoh
aya oncan matli inquemanā ncanni yas noca icamaoço nic ya
cauhhuac in thoc y onnemis noyol canca yonican y a hualla yyancoya
nolnamicoca nemih yendeyo ay yo.

Nichoca yaniquittoaya nicnonancayotlo maniquitta cuicanelhuayol aya ma
nic ya halaqui ya maya thoc quimmā mochhuia onnencanihngotl y
çan cateuc xochitl ahuiaca ipotocahuac mocepanoa yon toxochiuh a yye
ayaoo hui yoncanqui ya iztmolini yenocuie celia nohlatolhaquillo o
hua intoxochiuh ycac y quiapani ayao

Toleaca hua xochitl a huiac xeliuhhuic a ipoto aya inahuiyac popoma
tlin pixahuia oncan nineñenomi nicuicanitl yye ayao hui
yoncaquiya iztmolini yenocuie celia y

The letter continues, beseeching the Holy Father that after reading the results of the Process, he might deign to acclaim the apparition and the Image as miraculous.[22]

The enthusiastic hopes which the activities of 1666 had stirred up in the hearts of the Mexicans were not realized. Whether through neglect or other obstacles, no immediate response was given to the petition sent to the Holy See.[23] Almost one hundred years were to transpire before the valuable testimonies of 1666 would be used in the final approbation of the apparition by His Holiness Benedict XIV. In spite of this misfortune, the Apostolic Process would in time prove to be one of the strong foundation stones that would strengthen and stabilize the growing Guadalupan cult.

[22] *Ibid.*

[23] Vera, *Información Sobre la Milagrosa Aparición de la Santísima Virgen de Guadalupe Recibida en 1666–1723* (Amecameca, México: Imprenta Católica, 1889), p. 195.

★ CHAPTER FOUR

THE MIRACULOUS IMAGE

As legitimate tradition supported the historicity of the apparition of Tepeyac, many miracles attributed to the Blessed Virgin under her title of Guadalupe substantiate its supernatural origin. The historical basis of the cult was given greater depth by the early miracles which were to bear out the truth of the words spoken by Mary. The Author of all truth has definitively sanctioned the holiness and truth of the sacred Image by granting miraculous effects through its invocation. These innumerable marvels wrought by Our Lady of Guadalupe have sealed her cult throughout history with the sign of authenticity.

In the Office for the Feast of the Apparition, mention is made of the many miracles worked by Our Lady: ". . . *ingentíque abhinc quátuor sáeculis cólitur populórum ac miraculórum frequéntia.*" [1] In the original Office approved by His Holiness Benedict XIV in 1754, some specific miracles were described. Among these early miracles, three are outstanding: the resurrection of a Chichimeca Indian on December 26, 1531; the deliverance from destruction by the flood of 1629; and the cessation of the plague in 1737. [2] These three miraculous interventions of Our Lady are especially significant — the first because it occurred on the very day of the translation of the Image; the second and third because of their widespread effect. Pope Benedict XIV used these same three miracles in his Brief, *Non est equidem*, of May 25, 1754, to illustrate the constant tradition of miracles in the cult of the Virgin of Tepeyac. [3]

Although Our Lady had miraculously cured the dying Juan Bernardino, Juan Diego's uncle, at Tolpetlac on the morning of December 12, [4] the incident is usually known as the fifth apparition. It is the restoration to life of the Indian dancer on the day of the translation of the

---

[1] The seventh lesson in the Office of Matins for the Feast of Our Lady of Guadalupe, December 12.

[2] de la Rosa, p. 141.

[3] Vera, *Colección de Documentos Eclesiásticos de México* (Amecameca, 1887), II, 118.

[4] Becerra Tanco, p. 15.

Image to the first Shrine which is popularly called the "first miracle" wrought by the Virgin of Guadalupe.

On December 26, 1531, fifteen days after the first apparition, a solemn procession accompanied the sacred Image from the church to the crude adobe hermitage which had been built by the Indians some four miles outside of Mexico City on the site where Our Lady had stood: [5]

> On the very day on which the Holy Image was transferred, in a military festival which the Indians were celebrating . . . an arrow flew from a bow and pierced the throat of an Indian, casting him to the ground and wounding him to death. They took him with great cries and lamentations and placed him almost dead [completely dead, according to the oldest accounts] at the feet of the Holy Image of the Virgin, begging her intercession with faith and devotion. Our Lady did not wish the death of an Indian on this great day on which her Image was to be placed in its proper place for the salvation and happiness of the Indians, and so when the arrow was removed from the throat of the Indian, he returned to life and showed no sign of wound or scar.[6]

Mexico City, which has often suffered from destructive floods, experienced its longest, most general, and disastrous inundation in the year 1629. This crisis was to occasion the second major miracle attributed to our Blessed Mother's intervention. On the feast of Saint Matthew, September 21, 1629, the rain began to fall with incredible force. After thirty-six hours of continuous downpour, the entire city was flooded. By the sixteenth of October, thirty thousand Indians had lost their lives in the disaster, and of twenty thousand Spanish families, only four hundred survived.[7] The effects of the flood were widespread; "humidity, hunger, and the rotting of unburied corpses and animals caused pestilence."[8] In the midst of this tragedy the Archbishop of Mexico, Francisco Manso y Zúñiga, turned his eyes to Our Lady of Guadalupe. After consulting with the Viceroy and both Cathedral and Civil Chapters, he decided to remove the Image from its altar and bring it to the Cathedral in an effort to obtain the cessation of the flood by Our Lady's intercession: [9]

> They withdrew the Virgin from her altar after 108 years, . . . and installing her in the archbishop's boat, together with the most important personages in his retinue, they rowed to Mexico City. There was a great display of lights in all the vessels and music from bugles. . . . The choir of the Cathedral also sang psalms and hymns, but

[5] Velázquez, p. 251.
[6] Florencia, pp. 114–15.
[7] Velázquez, p. 256.
[8] Ibid., p. 257.
[9] Florencia, p. 120.

with more harmony than joy, because, although they were trustful in the company of the Virgin from whom they hoped for a remedy, they were not completely happy.[10]

The confidence of the people in their Patroness finally obtained the desired blessing; and although the flood did not recede immediately, the waters began to decline gradually. The city was saved and rebuilt, and the Virgin of Guadalupe was unanimously acclaimed by all as the deliverer of the city. And the incident was publicly and officially acknowledged as a miracle. As such, it was carefully recorded and communicated to Rome and Spain. On May 14, 1634, after the water had completely receded, the picture was triumphantly carried back to the Shrine.[11]

A little over a hundred years after saving the city of Mexico from destruction by water, Our Lady again manifested her power by delivering the whole nation from a strange malady. In August of 1736, an unknown fever accompanied by chills, nosebleeds, and spasms began to spread rapidly throughout the whole nation. It was calculated that over forty thousand succumbed in a short period of time.[12] A contemporary report certifies that in Toluca alone "in only three or four days more than one thousand Indians had perished."[13]

In the throes of this disaster, the Mexican people once again turned to Our Lady. This third outstanding miracle proved to be of great consequence since, after much prayer and reflection, it was decided to proclaim Our Lady of Guadalupe the Patroness of the Capital. This measure was enthusiastically accepted by the clergy, government officials, and by all the faithful. The Decree of Patronage was written by Juan Antonio Vizarrón y Egiarreta, Archbishop of Mexico; and on April 27, 1737, representatives of both the civil government and the Cathedral Chapter solemnly declared Our Lady of Guadalupe the Patroness of Mexico City.[14]

No sooner had the "vow" been ratified than the effects were palpably felt. Historians agree that the plague of 1737 was assuaged as soon as the Patronage was decreed. The miraculous intervention of the Virgin seems indubitable. Critical observers may object that a plague might disappear by natural means as suddenly as it had appeared. Only the conviction of a whole nation, that the cessation of the contagion was due to the intercession of our Blessed Mother, can refute such a belief.

[10] *Ibid.*
[11] Lee, p. 212.
[12] Velázquez, p. 279.
[13] Cabrera y Quintero, p. 412.
[14] Vera, *Notas del Compendio Histórico del Concilio III Mexicano* (México: Imprenta del Colegio Católico, 1879), II, 193.

For "that generation of Mexicans, and all generations since, declare that the decimating plague of 1737 was stopped by Our Lady of Guadalupe." [15] She who is an ever ready help in public and private calamities, "*praestissimum adversus publicas privatasque calamitatis praesidium*," [16] had once more shown herself to be a merciful Mother to the afflicted.

To these outstanding and official miracles may be added many others which are recorded in history as having been verified by reliable witnesses. The plague of *cocoliztli* in 1544, which had already killed twelve thousand Indians in a few days, was stayed by the faith manifested by a procession of six- and seven-year-old children who walked from Tlatilolco to Tepeyac doing penance and beseeching Our Lady for help.[17] And in 1565, the sailors of the threatened ship *San Lucas*, which was returning to Mexico from the Philippines, vowed to make a pilgrimage to the Shrine of Our Lady if they were saved. They reached their destination safely and kept their promise by carrying their one remaining sail to the hill of Tepeyac. Today a monument of the sail set on the hillside of Tepeyac commemorates the miracle.[18]

To catalogue the miraculous interventions of Our Lady since her apparition to the present day would require a lengthy and extensive research. The thousands of ex-votos, plaques, drawings, and offerings donated by the faithful to attest their gratitude and faith in her power cover many walls in the Basilica and publicly manifest the countless favors which the Virgin obtains for her children. These innumerable favors and the official miracles attributed to Mary of Guadalupe clearly reveal the truth and fecundity of the maternal promises first conveyed to Juan Diego in 1531 and faithfully fulfilled throughout the history of the Mexican nation.

Above and beyond all miracles, however, stands the Holy Image, which is in itself the greatest marvel. "The greatest, the most ancient and the most authorized miracle of Our Lady of Guadalupe is her Blessed Image which our eyes witness and which our hands touch." [19] This "living miracle" never ceases to be an object of wonder. Benedict XIV, the "Guadalupan Pope," exclaims of it in admiration:

> In it there is nothing that is not wonderful: a picture from flowers gathered in mid-winter on a soil entirely sterile and fit to bear only thorns; on a cloth so thin that through it as through a lattice the temple lay easily open to the eyes; and that after two centuries the

[15] Lee, p. 218.
[16] Office for the feast of December 12; the seventh lesson of Matins.
[17] Florencia, p. 115.
[18] García Gutiérrez, *Efemérides Guadalupanos* (México: Antigua Imprenta de Murguia, 1931), pp. 131–32.
[19] Florencia, pp. 136–37.

nitrate of the neighboring lakes which erodes silver, gold, and brass has not in the least injured its supreme beauty.[20]

It was this same pontiff who was presented with a copy of the original Image painted by Miguel Cabrera. Juan Francisco López, Procurator General of the Society of Jesus in Mexico, bestowed the painting with the following words: "Most Holy Father, behold the Mother of God, who has deigned to be the Mother of the Mexicans." Benedict XIV, deeply moved, fell to his knees before the Image and exclaimed the words of Psalm 147, "*Non fecit taliter omni nationi.*"[21] This eulogy from the Vicar of Christ has come down as the Guadalupan motto which proclaims to the world the uniqueness and wonder of the Sacred Image of Mary of Guadalupe.[22] To the sanction of the Sovereign Pontiff can be added the opinion of the Sacred Congregation regarding the miraculous nature of the Image.

In the Office of the Blessed Virgin of Guadalupe, the Congregation of Rites expressly mentions that the Holy Image appeared painted in an extraordinary fashion, *mirabiliter picta.*[23]

Artists and scientists have vied with one another in critical analyses of the Image. The most historical and well known work is that of Miguel Cabrera. This master artist headed a commission of artists chosen to examine the sacred picture in detail. The aim of the investigation, which opened on April 30, 1751, was twofold: to determine by close inspection if the work might possibly be one of human industry; to study the details in an effort to paint a perfect copy of the Image for His Holiness Benedict XIV.[24] The results of the observations of this commission are given in Cabrera's book entitled *Maravilla Americana*. The affirmation of the miraculous nature of the picture is even more evident in this work than in the Process of 1666:

> The plan of this Holy Picture is so singular — so perfectly accomplished and so manifestly marvelous, that I hold for certain that whoever has any knowledge of our art must at once declare it a marvelous portent . . . Every line and turn of it is so clearly a

[20] Vera, *Apuntamientos Históricos de los Concilios Provinciales Mexicanos y Privilegios de América* (México: 1893), p. 295.

[21] José Dávila y Arrillaga, *Continuación de la Historia de la Compañía de Jesús en Nueva España* (Puebla, México: Imprenta del Colegio Pío de Artes y Oficios, 1888), p. 114.

[22] It has been denied that Benedict XIV was the first to say the words, "*Non fecit* . . . ,*" in reference to Our Lady of Guadalupe as Father Florencia in 1670 had struck medals which carried the same inscription. "When it is said that Benedict XIV was the first to say the words we mean first in the order of authority, not first in the order of time" (Antícoli, p. 26).

[23] Antícoli, p. 34.

[24] Julián Tornel y Mendivil, *La Aparición de Nuestra Señora de Guadalupe de México* (Orizava [*sic*], México: José M. Naredo, 1849), I, 105.

miracle that there actually palpitates in the admirable work the supreme power of the Author.[25]

The analysis of the material of the Image revealed a wonderful phenomenon. The crude fabric which appears so rough has the texture of a soft silk on one side. The reverse side is always described as rough:

> What for the moment would excite wonder is the smoothness felt in this *ayate*; for, all the roughness which appears to the eye is, to the touch, converted into a soft smoothness like that of silk. This I have experienced on the repeated occasions on which I had the happiness of touching it, and certainly other *ayates* of the same kind do not enjoy this privilege.[26]

The artists all agreed that the material of the *ayate* was of such quality that, even if the climatic conditions had been favorable, "the material itself was enough to make it fall to pieces in a very short time." [27] In his observations Cabrera also points out the phenomenal durability of the cotton thread which joins the two pieces of *ayate* and which had resisted the weight of the two heavier pieces of cloth for centuries.[28]

Two of the most perplexing discoveries made by the artists were the lack of preparatory base in the picture and the media used in painting. The Process of 1666 had already affirmed that the colors are visible on both sides of the *ayate*, a fact which proves the absolute lack of a priming coat on the material. No human artist could have possibly painted on such a coarse burlap-like cloth without a preparatory base.[29] The other remarkable feature of the Holy Image is the fourfold medium which is discernible:

> One admires four types or modes of painting in Guadalupe; one in oil, one in gum coloring, one in water color, and one a labored tempera . . . I believe that until the Picture of Guadalupe appeared, no one could have imagined such a reality.[30]

The verdict of the examining artists stated that the head and hands of the Virgin are done in oil painting; the tunic, angel, and clouds in gum coloring; the mantle in water color; the background in labored tempera.[31]

Not only is the Holy Image wonderful in its origin and conservation,

[25] Miguel Cabrera, *Maravilla Americana* (México: Imprenta del Real y Más Antiguo Colegio de San Ildefonso, 1756), p. 6.

[26] *Ibid.*, p. 4.

[27] *Ibid.*, p. 2.

[28] *Ibid.*

[29] *Ibid.*, p. 5.

[30] *Ibid.*, p. 12.

[31] *Ibid.*

but it has also proved to be impervious to elements which by their nature should have destroyed it. On one occasion "when some silver-smiths were cleaning the frame, a bottle of nitric acid spilled over the cloth; the stain persists, but the cloth was neither destroyed nor dam-aged."[32] The corrosive acid lost its power when it touched the delicate cloth of the *tilma*.

The miraculous nature of the painting was again confirmed on No-vember 14, 1921, when a bomb was hidden at the foot of the Image in order to destroy it. This attempt by an anti-religious political faction proved futile. The marble of the altar was pulverized; the huge bronze crucifix above the altar was twisted out of shape, but the Image was not even slightly damaged.[33]

The history of the Sacred Image of Our Lady of Guadalupe, therefore, reflects a great fund of phenomenal facts of an objective nature which clearly attest to the supernatural origin of the painting. It is evident that the validity of the traditional belief became more firmly established by the remarkable facts that arose out of the disinterested investigations of the Image and the miracles attributed to the intercession of Mary of Guadalupe.

[32] Tornel y Mendivil, p. 127.
[33] Cuevas, p. 269.

☆

PART THREE

☆

☆

THE HOLY SEE AND THE

BLESSED VIRGIN OF GUADALUPE

CHAPTER FIVE

ECCLESIASTICAL APPROBATION

Having considered the historical bases of the cult of Our Lady of Guadalupe as provided by documentation, tradition, and miracles, it is now necessary to reflect briefly on the attitude of the Mexican hierarchy towards Our Lady in her wonderful apparition. It is very significant that the Mexican Bishops have without exception supported the divine origin of the cult during the troubled period of growth and development in the colonization of a new nation and in the establishment of a new religion.

Fray Juan de Zumárraga was only the first in a long line of New World prelates who unanimously affirmed the validity of the miraculous Image. There are no documents from the pen of this first privileged Bishop of Mexico which clearly reveal his attitude in regard to the miraculous happenings of 1531. In spite of his silence, which has been a point of controversy among many Guadalupan writers, reliable historians assert that the venerable Zumárraga was spontaneous in his response to Our Lady's desire "that a temple be built." [1]

Fray Alonso de Montúfar, the Dominican successor to Zumárraga, presided over two provincial councils; and the demonstration which he gave of his approbation of the miracle is the strongest that could be desired.[2] The following mandate concerning the expurgation of apocryphal images from the churches may be found in chapter thirty-four of the records of the First Provincial Council held in 1555:

> Que los visitadores [de los Obispos] en las iglesias y lugares píos que visitaren, vean y examinen bien las historias e imágenes que estan pintadas hasta aquí y las que hallaren apócrifas . . . los hagan quitar de tales lugares.[3]
>
> That the visitators [of the Bishops] see and examine well the stories and images painted in the churches and places of devotion which they visit; if any apocryphal ones be found . . . they should see to it that they are removed from these places.

[1] Velázquez, p. 251.
[2] Tornel y Mendivil, p. 142.
[3] Lorenzana, p. 92.

Instead of removing the Holy Image from its Shrine, Montúfar became the patron of the hermitage which he had embellished in 1554.[4] Throughout his episcopacy, he not only strongly defended the truth of the miraculous nature of the Image, but also strove to augment the cult of Our Lady among the faithful.

These first two bishops of the infant Mexican Church in New Spain gave the initial impetus to a cult that was to broaden and deepen with the passage of time. At the Fifth Provincial Council held in 1896, the Fathers of the Council once again demonstrated the constant fidelity of the hierarchy which had for more than three centuries safeguarded the Guadalupan tradition. Section No. 434 of the Council proceedings exhorts the pastors to inculcate a deeper devotion to Our Lady of Guadalupe among the faithful:

> Memoriam revocent miraculosam Beatissimae Virginis Maria de Guadalupe . . . Apparitionem quem constanti et antiqua traditione a maioribus accepimus.[5]

In the same Council the members "absolutely prohibit anyone to speak, write, or teach anything contrary to the apparition of the Holy Virgin of Guadalupe." [6]

One year prior to this important Council, eleven archbishops and twenty-eight bishops had assisted at the glorious coronation ceremony of October 12, 1895.[7] As the mitered witnesses of the prodigy of Tepeyac laid their croziers at the feet of the Most Holy Virgin, they solemnly testified to the belief of the Mexican Church in Our Lady of Guadalupe whom they proclaimed as its Queen.

The steadfast labors of the Mexican episcopate finally secured the attainment of the Holy See's approbation by their appeals which exercised a strong and vital influence. Throughout four centuries the solemn, unbroken episcopal voice has ever declared that:

> "The Most clean Mother of the True God" had appeared in the land; that from Mary's visit and words the definite conversion of the people dated. . . . Whatever else was forgotten, this was to be remembered: the Mother of God had specially come to declare herself their Mother and to leave her miraculous Picture in their custody.[8]

Admirably faithful to Our Lady's defense and zealous in seeking her glory, the Shepherds of the Church of Mexico have labored unceasingly to draw their flocks to the Virgin of Tepeyac who is their Mother.

[4] Tornel y Mendivil, p. 142.
[5] Quinto Concilio . . . , p. 123.
[6] Ibid., p. 125.
[7] Velázquez, p. 305.
[8] Lee, p. 64.

It must be recognized that the firm establishment of the cult in its native country effected by the unanimity of the Mexican Bishops was a necessary and logical step in obtaining the indispensable and definitive approbation of Rome. It will be noted in tracing the history of papal approbation that it is also singularly characterized by a unique acceptance on the part of the Sovereign Pontiffs.

The Blessed Virgin of Guadalupe has received unrivalled glory and remarkable support through the devotion of Christ's Vicars. Since the sixteenth century, at least twenty popes have directly or indirectly approved devotion to Mary of Guadalupe in her miraculous apparition at Tepeyac; and numerous pontifical decrees have showered indulgences, extraordinary privileges, and honors on her ever-growing cult.

Although the final solemn act of approbation was not given until the year 1754, the way had been prepared by pontifical documents dating back to the century of the apparition. The first papal recognition of the devotion to Our Lady of Guadalupe was manifested by the granting of indulgences to the hermitage, confraternities, and temples erected in her honor.

The earliest known testimonial of papal interest in the devout cult of the Mexican Virgin is found in a memorandum of 1575 written by Father Everardo Mercuriano, Provost General of the Society of Jesus, to Father Pedro Sánchez, Provincial of the Society in Mexico. This ancient document shows that His Holiness Gregory XIII had conferred an extension of indulgences previously given by the Holy See to the Hermitage of Guadalupe. It is of great importance since it proves that before 1575 temporal indulgences had been granted to the pilgrims who visited the hermitage: [9]

> This document is of tremendous significance since it proves that within an incredibly short time after its foundation, the Sanctuary of Guadalupe had been recognized by the Holy See as a repository of special grace.[10]

The first formal pontifical document still existing was issued in the seventeenth century by Pope Urban VIII in the granting of indulgences to the Confraternity of Our Lady of Guadalupe.[11] This first link in the glorious chain of Guadalupan papal documents was reinforced by Pope Innocent X, to whom Mexico had sent a copy of the original Image as a token of gratitude. This pontiff was the first person ever to receive a copy of the original, and the fact that he had it placed in his apostolic chambers shows that he personally venerated it.[12]

[9] Demarest and Taylor, p. 243.
[10] Pompa y Pompa, p. 147.
[11] García Gutiérrez, p. 147.
[12] Vera, *Apuntamientos* . . . , p. 290.

Later, on February 6, 1664, Alexander VII granted a plenary indulgence to all the faithful who visited the Sanctuary on the fourteenth of December; [13] and it was during his reign that medals were struck with the words, *Non fecit taliter omni nationi*.[14] This same pontiff, it will be recalled, received the petition "that the Apparition be canonized as miraculous and the day of the apparition be declared a holy day." [15]

In 1667, when petitioned for a proper Office for Our Lady of Guadalupe, Clement IX, the successor of Alexander VII, stated that such an Office seemed unnecessary since the Image of Our Lady represented the Immaculate Conception during whose octave the apparition had taken place. As a consolation for this disappointment, His Holiness allowed Mexico a plenary jubilee indulgence for December 12. There was a mistake in the date, however, and the document was returned for rectification. Because of the fact that Clement IX had died in the meantime, no further action was taken concerning the matter.[16]

A brief issued on January 7, 1675, by Pope Clement X granted many indulgences to the Confraternity of Our Lady of Guadalupe, which had been instituted in her Sanctuary approximately in 1673 or 1674.[17] The following pontiff, Innocent XI, approved the Guadalupan Confraternity that had been established at Santiago de Querétaro and joined it to the Archconfraternity of Christian Doctrine at the Basilica of Saint Peter.[18] In the brief *Ad augendam fidelium* of November 20, 1682, this same pontiff granted for fifteen years a plenary indulgence to "those who visit the Sanctuary during the Forty Hours' Devotion." [19]

Pope Innocent XII in the brief *Putatis et caritatis opera*, which was issued on September 5, 1691, approved and confirmed the congregation of secular clergy which had been founded in Querétaro in 1659.[20] The briefs *Considerantes* of February 3, 1702, of Clement XI and *Ad augendam* of August 20, 1722, of Innocent XIII, continued the blessings of the Holy See on the cult of Our Lady of Guadalupe.[21]

Great was the jubilation of the Mexican nation when His Holiness Benedict XIII directed the Bull for the erection of the Collegiate Church at Guadalupe to the Archbishop of Mexico, Francisco José Lanciego y

[13] The Pope had been misinformed on the date of the feast. Later when he asked that the twelfth be made a holy day, the mistake was rectified. Frances P. Keyes, *The Grace of Guadalupe* (New York: Julian Messner, Inc., 1946), p. 128.
[14] Demarest and Taylor, p. 244.
[15] Lucio Villanueva, *La Inmaculada del Tepeyac* (México, 1945), p. 72.
[16] Velázquez, p. 77.
[17] Vera, *Apuntamientos* . . . , p. 291.
[18] Joseph Zelaa e Hidalgo, *Glorias de Querétaro* (México: Imprenta por D. Mariano de Zúñiga, 1803), p. 126.
[19] Vera, *Apuntamientos* . . . , p. 291.
[20] *Ibid.*, p. 292.
[21] *Ibid.*, p. 293.

Equiluz on February 9, 1725. On nominating the church to be made a
Colegiata Insignis, he exalted the Sanctuary as a place of pilgrimage:

> In qua prodigiosa illa ejusdem Beatae Mariae Virginis de Guadalupe
> nuncupatae satis decentis asservatur pieque colitur Imago, ad quam
> Christifidelium illuc undique peregrinantium pro obtinenda a tam
> grandi misericordiarum et gratiarum Matre.[22]

This decree of Benedict XIII, however, was not put into effect, for the
Sanctuary of Guadalupe remained a simple church. On July 15, 1746,
Pope Benedict XIV confirmed and revalidated the dispositions of his
predecessors on the erection of the Collegiate Church with the Bull
Divinae gratiae munere.[23] In October of the year 1750, the exultant de-
votees of Our Lady of Guadalupe rejoiced in the final erection of the
Collegiate Church. Only the official recognition of the already sworn
Patronage of the Virgin of Tepeyac was lacking.

The pontiff who was at last to grant this long-awaited privilege was
the great Benedict XIV, a man "especially distinguished by liturgical,
doctrinal, and historical research and decisiveness."[24] It is noteworthy
that this much-loved Pope, who was inclined to be conservative in regard
to innovations, was to become the most active in furthering the cause
of Our Lady of Guadalupe.

Father Francisco López, S.J., was the envoy chosen to carry the petition to His Holiness Benedict XIV. After the formal supplication had
been made, it was discovered that certain indispensable documents
were missing. When the Archives of the Congregation of Rites were
searched for the required proceedings of the Apostolic Process of 1666,
the necessary documents could not be found. Ready to return to Mexico,
Father López providentially discovered a work which contained the
entire account of the Process. This work, entitled *The Historical Account of the Admirable Apparition of the Most Holy Virgin of God
under the Title of Nuestra Señora de Guadalupe which took place in
Mexico in 1531,* was written in 1681 by a Roman prelate, Anastasio
Nicoselli. It had been presented in that year to the Congregation and
had been archived under No. 3971. It is understandable that nothing
ever came of this document since the apparent indifference of Rome
was founded on the maxim that the Holy See does not easily open its
doors to canonize miraculous images.[25] When the missing information
was presented to the Holy Father, he immediately and spontaneously

---

[22] Archivos de la Basílica de Santa María de Guadalupe, Original Bull of February 9, 1725, *Suma dispositiones illius.*

[23] Archivos de la Basílica de Santa María de Guadalupe, Original Bull of July
15, 1746, *Divinae gratiae munere.*

[24] Lee, p. 28.

[25] *Ibid.,* p. 34.

granted the request of the Mexican hierarchy by his famous brief *Non est equidem* of May 25, 1754.[26]

The pontifical sanction of Pope Benedict XIV is of utmost importance since it clearly defines the position of the Church in regard to the apparition; it harmoniously unites historical and doctrinal data; and it "confirms in brief the tradition of the Mexican Church about the apparition of the Virgin Mother of God on the hill of Tepeyac."[27] The three motives for granting the desired privileges are contained in the solemn act of approbation of May 1754:

> We, by these words, confirm with Our Apostolic Authority, the election of the Most Holy Virgin Mary under the invocation of Guadalupe . . . for the greater glory of Almighty God, for the furtherance of divine worship, and for the honor of the Virgin Mary.[28]

Benedict XIV based his decisive approbation on the sources that have been considered in previous chapters; the constant tradition of the miracle; the authentic Indian documents; the testimony of the witnesses of 1666; and the miracles worked through the intercession of the Virgin of Tepeyac.[29]

The composition and form of the brief *Non est equidem* make it not only the significant word of the Vicar of Christ, but also a comprehensive synthesis of the history and doctrine of the cult of Our Lady of Guadalupe. The brief is divided into three main parts. The historical section contains the account of the apparition as written by Father López and the proper Mass and Office which had been presented for approval. The confirmation of the National Patronage,[30] the decree of the Congregation of Rites approving the Mass and Office, and the solemn confirmation made by the Sovereign Pontiff in his own name make up the contents of the doctrinal section. As a consequence of the antecedent parts, the third section enumerates the privileges and indulgences conceded:[31]

> By this we approve and confirm with Apostolic Authority the election of the Most Blessed Virgin under the title of Guadalupe as patroness and protectress of New Spain . . . We approve and con-

[26] Sacerdote de la Compañía de Jesús, *El Magisterio de la Iglesia y la Virgen de Guadalupe* (Querétaro: Imprenta de la Escuela de Artes, 1892), p. 43.

[27] Sacerdote de la Compañía de Jesús, *La Santísima Virgen de Guadalupe en México* (México: Tip. y Lit. La Europa, 1897), II, 106.

[28] Vera, *Colección* . . . , II, 120.

[29] Anon., *Santa María de Guadalupe* . . . , pp. 253-55.

[30] On July 2, 1757, at the petition of Ferdinand VI of Spain, Benedict XIV extended the Mass and Office of Our Lady of Guadalupe to all the Spanish dominions. Dávila y Arrillaga, p. 117.

[31] Sacerdote de la Compañía de Jesús, *La Santísima Virgen*, pp. 106-7.

firm the Office and Mass here inserted and we declare, decree, and command that the Mother of God, called Holy Mary of Guadalupe, be recognized, invoked, and venerated.[32]

It seemed that with these generous blessings, Benedict XIV had poured out on the cult of Guadalupe all the treasures of Rome. His successors, nevertheless, continued to extend the favors already bestowed. His Holiness Clement XIII granted for a period of fifteen years a plenary indulgence to all who visited the Collegiate Church of Guadalupe during the first three days of the year.[33] The two remaining eighteenth-century popes, Clement XIV and Pius VI, prolonged the spiritual favors on behalf of the devotees of the Virgin of Guadalupe. The latter not only bestowed indulgences on those who visited the Shrine itself, but also accorded the same graces on the twelfth of each month to anyone visiting any church where Our Lady of Guadalupe was venerated.[34]

Pope Pius VII, whose pontificate opened the nineteenth century, permanently attached the Shrine of Guadalupe to the Basilica of St. John Lateran on May 26, 1805. In a later mandate during the same year, he authorized the celebration of the votive Mass in honor of Our Lady of Guadalupe in her Sanctuary on every Saturday of the year, even on the days which ranked as second-class feasts and during octaves.[35]

The succeeding pontiffs, Leo XII, Pius VIII, and Gregory XVI, all continued to accord indulgences and blessings to the Guadalupan cult. The favor with which Gregory XVI looked upon the devotion to the Mexican Virgin is evident from his brief of May 17, 1839, in which he diminished the number of feast days celebrated in Mexico. Among the excepted feasts are "la Concepción [de la Virgen María] y su aparición en Guadalupe." [36]

Pope Pius IX is also venerated as one of the great Guadalupan popes:

> The concessions he granted were many, but notable among the graces granted by him and the actions which reveal his devotion were his dedication of a Chapel to Our Lady of Guadalupe in the Church of San Nicolás in Carcere,[37] and his approbation of the Military

---

[32] Sacerdote de la Compañía de Jesús, *El Magisterio*, p. 43.

[33] Vera, *Apuntamientos* . . . , p. 297.

[34] *Ibid.*, p. 298.

[35] *Ibid.*, pp. 299-300.

[36] Pompa y Pompa, p. 154.

[37] On February 28, 1797, His Eminence Julio M. de la Somaglia, Titular Cardinal of Santa Sabina and Vicar General of His Holiness Pius VI, issued the decree sanctioning the miraculous movement of the eyes of the Roman copy of the Virgin of Guadalupe in the Church of San Nicolás in Carcere during the month of July in 1796. Vera, *Apuntamientos* . . . , p. 299.

Order [38] which bore the name of Guadalupe and to whose members was granted a plenary indulgence *in articulo mortis*.[39]

In his brief *Nedum tituli honoris* of April 4, 1854, the Sovereign Pontiff approved the re-establishment of the Military Order of Guadalupe:

> We confirm with Our Apostolic Authority . . . the Mexican Order of Knights named for the Blessed Virgin Mary of Guadalupe as it is now re-established.[40]

These popes manifested their interest in the cult of Our Lady of Guadalupe, but the pontiff whose name is most closely associated with Guadalupe after Benedict XIV is Leo XIII. This pope, who had said, "When I think of Mexico, I think at the same time of the Virgin of Guadalupe," [41] officially stamped the cult of Our Lady in Mexico with the seal of authenticity in a measure that is unrivalled. Benedict XIV had given the cult so high an ecclesiastical standing that his successors' legislation seemed limited, but the "light, strong hand of Leo XIII has magically touched the sacred subject, and has beautified what was already very beautiful." [42]

The pontiff's special love for Mexico and its Queen is evident from the words spoken by him to the first Mexican pilgrims to Rome in 1888:

> Notable was the devotion of your forefathers. . . . Of this devotion, to speak no further, the pious institutions they founded, the sacred monuments, the sumptuous churches erected in your cities, bear witness. Among them it is scarcely necessary to mention the famous Sanctuary of Our Lady of Guadalupe, from which the most august Virgin, venerated with such special devotion by the Mexican people, seems to keep your country under her sweet tutelage and to guard it lovingly in the shade of her protection.[43]

Seven years later on February 26, 1895, when again addressing a group of pilgrims from Mexico, he read a Latin distich which he himself had written in honor of Our Lady of Guadalupe. These lines were set to music and were sung at the Offertory of the Mass during the solemn coronation ceremonies of 1895.[44] Today this tribute of the great pope is inscribed in bronze at the feet of the Holy Image. It reads:

[38] First established by the Emperor Iturbide and later renewed by Maximilian. Demarest and Taylor, p. 248.

[39] Pompa y Pompa, p. 154.

[40] Jesús García Gutiérrez, "Pío IX y la Orden Militar de Guadalupe," *Divulgación Histórica*, II (1940), 142.

[41] Pompa y Pompa, p. 159.

[42] Lee, p. 48.

[43] Demarest and Taylor, p. 248.

[44] *Ibid.*, p. 198.

Mexicus, hic populus, mira sub Imagine gaudet
Te colere alma parens praesidioque frui
Per Te sic vigeat felix, teque auspice Cristi
Immotam servet firmior usque fidem.

Leo P.P. XIII
Imagini Augustae Mariae Dominae Nostrae
Guadalupensis in Mexico subscribendum
diem xxvi Feb. an MDCCCXCV
Romae ex aedibus Vatic.[45]

The English rendition as found in *The Dark Virgin* is as follows:

Happy in the possession of Thy Miraculous Image
The Mexican people rejoice in Thy sway,
And firm in their faith and Thy patronage, pray
Thy son's Will will always govern their land.[46]

Likewise memorable in Guadalupan history is the brief of February 8, 1887, in which His Holiness conceded the coronation of the Image as requested by the Mexican hierarchy.[47] The ceremony was delayed for eight years while the Sanctuary was fittingly prepared for so glorious an event. Finally, on October 12, 1895, in the name of Pope Leo XIII, the Archbishop of Mexico, Don Próspero María Alarcón y Sánchez, placed the jewelled crown of gold above the Sacred Image.[48] With this solemn act, Mary of Guadalupe was officially recognized as Queen of Mexico.

In 1894 the Congregation of Rites issued the approbatory decree for the new Office of the feast of December 12. On this occasion Leo XIII expressed his deep sentiments of love for Our Lady in the letter *Perlibenti* dated August 2, which he addressed to the archbishops and bishops of Mexico:

Magna ideo caritate Mexicanam nationem per vos hortamus, ut reverentiam et amorem eius sic tueatur perinde ac decus eximium et praestantissimorum fortem bonorum.[49]

The teaching and sentiments of Pope Leo XIII in regard to their Virgin have brought this great pontiff very close to the hearts of the Mexican people. During the years of persecution which shortly followed his pontificate, the Catholics of Mexico were sustained and encouraged by the promise given to them by this Vicar of Christ:

With regard especially to the Catholic faith . . . let all hold for certain that it will last among you in all its purity and firmness, as long as this devotion, worthy of your ancestors, remains constant.[50]

[45] Basilica of Our Lady of Guadalupe, Mexico City.
[46] Demarest and Taylor, p. 198.   [49] AAS, XIV, 278.
[47] Vera, *Colección* . . . , I, 689.   [50] *Quinto Concilio* . . . , p. 125.
[48] Velázquez, p. 300.

The pontiffs of the twentieth century have continued to honor Our Lady of Guadalupe. Saint Pius X extended the dominions under the special patronage of the Mexican Virgin by declaring her the Patroness of all Latin America on August 24, 1910.[51] On June 23, 1908, he had raised the Collegiate Church to the rank of a Minor Basilica and in the corresponding brief declared:

> Among the most famous sanctuaries of the Catholic world, that which exists in Mexico in honor of the Virgin of Guadalupe should be numbered in all right and justice.[52]

Benedict XV, the Pope of Peace, exclaimed as he crowned a copy of the Holy Image in Rome, "Yes, the Virgin of Guadalupe is the Pope's Patroness." [53] In the reign of Pius XI, the 400th anniversary of the apparition of Our Lady in Mexico was celebrated. On December 12, 1931, the Archbishop of Guadalajara sang a Pontifical Mass in the papal chapel of the Vatican in the presence of His Holiness. Later in the day, a copy of the Sacred Image was carried in a solemn procession through the streets of the Eternal City. Pius XI also extended the patronage of Our Lady of Guadalupe to the Philippines and in 1938 proclaimed a Holy Year in her honor.[54]

During the reign of Pius XII there was a great surge of devotion to Our Lady. On October 12, 1945, the day which marked the fiftieth anniversary of the coronation by Leo XIII, the Holy Image was crowned anew in the name of the Holy Father. In a radio address which is memorable for its beauty as well as for its doctrine, His Holiness Pius XII declared the Most Holy Virgin of Guadalupe to be Empress of America.[55] With unsurpassed eloquence, the Vicar of Christ's voice resounded through the Temple of Our Lady in the language of her own children:

> Nos colocamos hoy de nuevo sobre tus sienes la corona que pone para siempre bajo tu poderoso patrocinio la pureza y la integridad de la santa fe en Méjico y en todo el Continente Americano. Porque estamos cierto de que mientras Tú seas reconcida como Reina y como Madre, América y Méjico se han salvado.[56]
>
> Today we once again put upon your brow the crown that forever places under your powerful patronage the purity and integrity of the holy faith in Mexico and on all the American continent. Because we are certain that as long as you are recognized as Queen and Mother, America and Mexico will be saved.

[51] Pompa y Pompa, p. 159.
[52] Ibid.
[53] Ibid.
[54] Ibid.
[55] AAS, XII, 267ff.
[56] Ibid.

The devotion and love for the Mexican Virgin which inspired Pius XII was manifest also in the reign of the recent Vicar of Christ. It is evident that His Holiness John XXIII continued the remarkable tradition of papal support in regard to Our Lady of Guadalupe. Shortly after his election he placed all the works of the Episcopal Commission of Latin America under the protection of the Latin Virgin.[57] And on October 12, 1960, he declared a Marian Year for Mexico. One year later, the Holy Father addressed the faithful who had assembled in the Basilica of Our Lady for the solemn closing of this year dedicated to Mary. As he once more confirmed with Apostolic Authority the miraculous nature of the Holy Image, he urged the Mexican nation to an ever greater confidence in the protection of their Patroness and Queen.[58]

During four centuries of trial and growth, the cult of Our Lady of Guadalupe has become the solid bulwark of the Catholic faith in Mexico due to the exceptional support both of the Mexican hierarchy and the Sovereign Pontiffs. The much-loved tradition of the miracle of Tepeyac which for years was devoutly and rationally accepted is today unquestionably believed on the approving authority of the Holy See.

[57] Interview with Monsignor Gregorio Aguilar, former Rector and Acting Abbot of the Basilica of Our Lady of Guadalupe.

[58] Archivos de la Basílica de Santa María de Guadalupe, Radio Message of Pope John XXIII, October 12, 1961.

★
★ CHAPTER SIX
★

THEOLOGICAL REFLECTIONS ON THE GUADALUPAN MESSAGE

Having once established the validity of the tradition and historicity of Our Lady's apparition at Tepeyac, it now remains to reflect, if only for a moment, on the words spoken by the Blessed Virgin in her visitation. This heavenly message is worthy of an extensive theological analysis. The present concern, however, will involve only certain brief reflections pertinent to the scope of this study in regard to this aspect of the words of Our Lady of Guadalupe.

The truth of the Guadalupan message has always been implicit in the mind of the Church. In proclaiming Our Lady of Guadalupe Patroness of Mexico and in granting the accompanying indulgences and privileges, the Holy See concomitantly approved the miraculous nature of the apparition and of Our Lady's words. For in approving the cult, the Church necessarily sanctioned the doctrine which the apparition represents:

> The object of the cult must be undoubtedly certain and based on truth, even though it is not necessarily a certainty of divine faith. It must at least be supported by the certainty of theological principles.[1]

The purpose of this chapter is to show the theological soundness of the message of Our Lady of Guadalupe. The historical legacy of the words spoken by the Blessed Virgin on the hill of Tepeyac is replete with theological principles. Three great prerogatives are manifestly asserted in the dialogue between Mary and the Indian neophyte: the divine maternity of the Virgin; her spiritual motherhood; and her role as Mediatrix of all graces.

The words which our Lady uses to identify herself in this apparition affirm the first Marian truth in the theological order, her divine

[1] Sacerdote de la Compañía de Jesús, *El Magisterio de la Iglesia* . . . , pp. 69-70.

motherhood. She explicitly states that she is the Mother of God. "I am the perfect and eternal Virgin Holy Mary, Mother of the true God through whom everything lives . . . ."[2] With these words Mary proclaims her greatest prerogative and the *raison d'être* of all her other privileges. The divine maternity, based as it is on the hypostatic union, is the supreme glory of Mary and the primary reason for her election. From this union of the divine nature with the human nature in the Person of the Word, it necessarily follows that in giving birth to Jesus, Mary gave birth to the eternal God. The mystery of God's predilection for Mary has placed her above all other creatures. Saint Thomas attributes a certain infinite dignity to this unique privilege of the Blessed Virgin:

> . . . et Beata Virgo ex hoc quod est Mater Dei, habent quandam dignitatem infinitam, ex bono infinito quod est Deus. Et ex hac parte non potest aliquid fieri melius eis, sicut non potest aliquid melius esse Deo.[3]

In her manifestation at Tepeyac, our Lady demonstrates how highly she esteems this singular dignity of the divine maternity.[4] Having announced her glorious title in the first apparition, she again identifies herself as the Mother of God in the second visit to the Indian: *Santa María in ninantzin Teotl Dios.*[5] With this all important truth firmly established, our Lady then enumerates the promises which proceed from it.

Just as the divine maternity is related to the hypostatic union, the spiritual motherhood of Mary proceeds from the dogma of the divine motherhood. In conceiving Jesus, the Head of the Mystical Body, Mary necessarily became the spiritual mother of His members. From the instant of His conception, Mary carried in her womb Christ united to the members of His Mystical Body.[6] Such is the teaching of Pius X in his encyclical of February 2, 1904, *Ad diem illum*:

> Already in the Virgin's chaste womb, Christ joined to Himself a spiritual body formed of all those who were to believe in Him; and it can be said that bearing Jesus in her womb, Mary also bore there all those whose life was included in that of the Savior's. And thus

---

[2] Garibay, p. 194.

[3] *Summa Theologiae*, I, q. 25, a. 6, ad 4.

[4] It is interesting to note the appearance of our Lady at this point in history since one of the main heresies of the Protestant Reformation was the denial of the divine maternity. It is also notable that the apparition of 1531 marked the 1100th anniversary of the Council of Ephesus in 431 when the title of *Theotokos* was solemnly attributed to the Blessed Virgin.

[5] Torroella, No. 41.

[6] Emil Neubert, S.M., *Mary in Doctrine* (Milwaukee: The Bruce Publishing Company, 1953), p. 45.

we are united to Christ and as the Apostle says, "We are members
of His body and of His flesh and of His bones" (Eph. 5:30).[7]

In the memorable phrase of *Mystici Corporis Christi,* Pius XII main-
tained that "she who corporally was the Mother of our Head, through
the added title of pain and glory, became spiritually the Mother of His
members."[8] This truth was directly and emphatically stated by our
Lady in the apparitions of Tepeyac: *"Yo soy vuestra madre misericor-
diosa."*[9]

In declaring herself to be a merciful Mother, Mary subsequently defines her activity in four ways which are essentially maternal: to love,
to compassionate, to help, and to defend:

> Here will I show, manifest, and give
> all my love: *notetlazotlaliz*
> my compassion: *noteicnoittaliz*
> my help: *notepalehuiliz*
> my protection: *notemanahuiliz*[10]

Having proclaimed herself a mother, our Lady then specifies those
whom this maternity embraces: "I am your merciful Mother — yours
and all those who live united in this land."[11] From these words it is
evident that Mary was speaking not only to the Indian neophyte and
his brethren, but also to the European inhabitants of the New World.
An exact translation of the expression, *In ixquichtin in nican tlalpan
ancepantlaca,*[12] clearly states that Mary is the Mother of all the dwellers
in the land in which she chose to reveal her clemency. But the full impact
of her appeal is realized in the claim to be the universal Mother of all
men:

> Mucho quiero y con intensidad deseo que en este lugar me levanten
> un templo. Allí ostentaré, haré exhibición, daré todo mi amor, mi
> compasión, mi ayuda, mi defensa de los hombres. Yo soy vuestra
> madre misericordiosa, de ti y de todos vosotros, los que vivís unidos
> en esta tierra, *y de todos los demás variados géneros de personas,*
> los que son mis amantes, los que claman a mí, los que me buscan, los
> que en mí tienen confianza. Allí he de oír su llanto, su tristeza, para
> remediar, para aliviar todos sus múltiples dolores, necesidades in-
> fortunios.[13]

> Deeply and intensely do I desire that a temple be raised here. Here I

[7] ASS, XXXVI, 453.
[8] AAS, XXXV, 247ff.
[9] Garibay, p. 194.
[10] *Ibid.,* p. 196.
[11] *Ibid.,* p. 195.
[12] *Ibid.,* p. 196: "Of all those who live united in this land."
[13] Ibid., pp. 194–95. (Italics mine.)

shall show, manifest, and give all my love, my compassion, my help, and my protection to mankind. I am your merciful mother; yours, and all those who live united in this land; and of all other peoples who are my loving ones, who cry to me, who seek me, and who trust in me. Here I shall listen to their weeping and sadness in order to remedy and alleviate their many sorrows, needs, and miseries.

Equally maternal are the conditions upon which our Lady bases her loving protection. To claim her help and call upon the Virgin of Guadalupe, her children must simply need her:

> They must love her: *notetlazotlacahuan*
> They must call upon her for help: *notech motzatzilia*
> They must seek her: *nech temoa*
> They must place confidence in her: *notechmotemachilia*[14]

There can be no doubt that the Blessed Virgin was intent on making it clear to Juan Diego, and through him to all men, that she is primarily and essentially a loving Mother:

> In accord with the general belief that Mary is the Mother of Mercy, we find in the text of the history of the Tepeyac revelation, the confirmation that Mary is *Mater Misericordiae, Virgo Clemens*, as the voice of the Church proclaims.[15]

The relationship between the universal Mother of love and those encompassed by this spiritual maternity brings the third great prerogative of Mary into perspective. The Church attributes a twofold activity to the Blessed Virgin: that of having co-operated in the redemption of men in union with her Son, although under a lesser title; that of distributing to mankind the graces of redemption.[16] Mary, Mother of God and spiritual Mother of men, is ever at the side of Jesus interceding for her children:

> Her mediation, far from diminishing that of Christ, results from it and seems to complete it: it is carried out under Christ and in union with Christ from whom it receives all its efficacy.[17]

Since she shares this double role with Jesus the Mediator, our Blessed Mother is rightly known as the Mediatrix of all graces. Pius X extols this truth with clarity and precision:

> We do not deny that the distribution of such benefits is the sole and private right of Christ . . . nevertheless, by that participation in suffering and labors of Mother and Son, it was granted to the Holy

---

[14] *Ibid.*, p. 197.
[15] *Ibid.*, p. 196.
[16] Neubert, p. 80.
[17] *Ibid.*, p. 72.

> Virgin to be with her only Son the most powerful Mediatrix and
> Redemptrix . . . Christ is the fountain: Mary is the aqueduct.[18]

As Mediatrix of all graces, the Blessed Virgin of Guadalupe appeals
for confidence in her power as Mother of God and co-redemptrix with
Christ. "Am I not your wellspring of grace? . . . Is there anything else
that you lack?"[19] Our Lady, in administering the treasures of the Sav-
ior's merits, promises to do what only an all-powerful mother could
accomplish. The Queen of Heaven declares to Juan Diego, to the
Mexican people, and to the world the truth of her unfailing protection
and help:

> Mary, in her apparition on Tepeyac, declares herself Mother of grace
> for the entire world, a wellspring of supernatural health and help
> in the things of this world . . . In truth, to those who sincerely
> invoke her as advocate of mankind, who have devotion to her, she
> will give her help, she who is the Mother of God: in truth, she will
> help greatly and show much compassion for those who love her,
> as though they walk under her shadow and under her protection.[20]

Thus it may be said that the historical fact of the words of our Lady
of Guadalupe fully concords with the fundamental principles of Marian doctrine. Our Lady's own words establish the theological criteria
of the miracle.

The scope of this book has been limited principally to a systematic
analysis of the historical documentation concerning the heavenly apparition at Tepeyac. A retrospective glance at the body of information that has been presented shows how the two separate fields of
analytical historical investigation plus the proceedings and approbation of the Church merged forces to form the valid foundation of the
Guadalupan miracle. To this framework of external corroboration
furnished by historical and ecclesiastical sources may now be added
the theological principles which impart the final solidarity to the cult
of our Lady of Guadalupe. The wealth of objective bases which support the cult can only serve to engender a deeper and more fruitful
faith.

The miracle of Tepeyac is as living a reality today as it was at the
time of its manifestation four centuries ago. The main elements of the apparition and the cult, the Image and the message of our Lady, remain
a bulwark of faith that has borne the test of time and investigation.
It is significant that the apparitions of the Blessed Virgin occurred at
a time when a symbol of unity was needed to stabilize the conflict of

[18] ASS, XXXVI, 454.
[19] Garibay, p. 199.
[20] Ibid., p. 202.

two opposing cultures and religions. The recent popes have acknowledged this powerful role of Holy Mary of Guadalupe by their fervent appeals to the peoples of this continent. In the present world conflict, the Catholics of the Western Hemisphere are exhorted to be united in peace and oneness under the mantle of stars of their common Mother. The maternal intercession and incomparable Image remain the symbol of hope and unity for the nations of this continent as the eyes of the faithful continue to return the loving gaze of the Most Holy Virgin Mary of Guadalupe, Queen of Mexico and Empress of the Americas.

APPENDIX

THE MIRACULOUS APPARITION OF THE BELOVED
VIRGIN MARY, OUR LADY OF GUADALUPE,
AT TEPEYACAC, NEAR MEXICO CITY
Luis Lazo de la Vega, 1649

Herein is told, in all truth, how by a great miracle the illustrious
Virgin, Blessed Mary, Mother of God, our Lady, appeared anew, in
the place known as Tepeyacac.

She appeared first to an Indian named Juan Diego; and later her
divine Image appeared in the presence of the first Bishop of Mexico,
Don Fray Juan de Zumárraga; also there are told various miracles
which have been done. It was ten years after the beginning of bringing
water from the mountain of Mexico, when the arrow and the shield
had been put away, when in all parts of the country there was tran-
quillity which was beginning to show its light, and faith and knowledge of Him was being taught through whose favor we have our being, who is the only true God.

In the year 1531, early in the month of December, it happened that
an humble Indian, called Juan Diego, whose dwelling, it is said, was
in Quahutítlan, although for divine worship he pertained to Tlatilolco,
one Saturday very early in the morning, while he was on his way to
divine worship according to his custom, when he had arrived near the
top of the hill called Tepeyacac, as it was near dawn, he heard above
the hill a singing like that when many choice birds sing together, their
voices resounding as if echoing throughout the hills; he was greatly
rejoiced; their song gave him rapture exceeding that of the bell-bird
and other rare birds of song.

Juan Diego stopped to wonder and said to himself: "Is it I who
have this good fortune to hear what I hear? Or am I perhaps only
dreaming? Where am I? Perhaps this is the place the ancients, our
forefathers, used to tell about — our grandfathers — the flowery land,
the fruitful land? Is it perchance the earthly paradise?"

And while he was looking towards the hilltop, facing the east, from which came the celestial song, suddenly the singing stopped and he heard someone calling as if from the top of the hill, saying: "Juan." Juan Diego did not dare to go there where he was being called; he did not move, perhaps in some way marvelling; yet he was filled with great joy and delight, and then, presently, he began to climb to the summit where he was called.

And, when he was nearing it, on the top of the peak he saw a lady who was standing there who had called him from a distance, and, having come into her presence, he was struck with wonder at the radiance of her exceeding great beauty, her garments shining like the sun; and the stones of the hill, and the caves, reflecting the brightness of her light were like precious gold; and he saw how the rainbow clothed the land so that the cactus and other things that grew there seemed like celestial plants, their leaves and thorns shining like gold in her presence. He made obeisance and heard her voice, her words, which rejoiced him utterly when she asked, very tenderly, as if she loved him: "Listen, xocoyote [1] mio, Juan, where are you going?"

And he replied: "My Holy One, my Lady, my Damsel, I am on my way to your house at Mexico-Tlatilulco; I go in pursuit of the holy things which our priests teach us."

Whereupon She told him, and made him aware of her divine will, saying: "You must know, and be very certain in your heart, my son, that I am truly the eternal Virgin, holy Mother of the True God, through whose favor we live, the Creator, Lord of heaven, and the Lord of the earth. I very much desire that they build me a church here, so that in it I may show and may make known and give all my love, my mercy and my help and my protection — I am in truth your merciful mother — to you and to all the other people dear to me who call upon me, who search for me, who confide in me; here I will hear their sorrow, their words, so that I may make perfect and cure their illnesses, their labors, and their calamities. And so that my intention may be made known, and my mercy, go now to the episcopal palace of the Bishop of Mexico and tell him that I send you to tell him how much I desire to have a church built here, and tell him very well all that you have seen and all that you have heard; and be sure in your heart that I will pay you with glory and you will deserve much that I will repay you for your weariness, your work, which you will bear diligently doing what I send you to do. Now hear my words, my dear son, and go and do everything carefully and quickly."

[1] *Xocoyote*: This Nahuatl word is variously translated into Spanish as if it were "my little son," "my son," "my dear son," "smallest of my sons," etc. *Xocoyota* is the form for daughter.

Then he humbled himself before her and said: "My Holy One, my Lady, I will go now and fulfill your commandment."

And straightway he went down to accomplish that with which he was charged, and took the road that leads straight to Mexico.

And when he had arrived within the city, he went at once to the episcopal palace of the Lord Bishop, who was the first [Bishop] to come, whose name was Don Fray Juan de Zumárraga, a religious of St. Francis. And having arrived there, he made haste to ask to see the Lord Bishop, asking his servants to give notice of him. After a good while they came to call him, and the Bishop advised them that he should come in; and when he had come into his presence, he knelt and made obeisance, and then after this he related the words of the Queen of Heaven, and told besides all that he had seen and all that he had heard. And [the Bishop] having heard all his words and the commandment as if he were not perfectly persuaded, said in response:

"My son, come again another time when we can be more leisurely; and I will hear more from you about the origin of this; I will look into this about which you have come, your will, your desire."

And he departed with much sorrow because he had not been able to convince him of the truth of his mission.

Thereupon he returned that same day and went straightway to the hill where he had seen the Queen of Heaven, who was even then standing there where he had first seen Her, waiting for him, and he, having seen Her, made obeisance, kneeling upon the ground, and said:

"My Holy One, most noble of persons, my Lady, my Xocoyota, my Damsel, I went there where You sent me; although it was most difficult to enter the house of the Lord Bishop, I saw him at last, and in his presence I gave him your message in the way You instructed me; he received me very courteously, and listened with attention; but he answered as if he could not be certain and did not believe; he told me: Come again another time when we can be at leisure, and I will hear you from beginning to end; I will look into that about which you come, what it is you want and ask me for. He seemed to me, when he answered, to be thinking perhaps that the church You desire to have made here was perchance not Your will, but a fancy of mine. I pray You, my Holy One, my Lady, my Daughter, that any one of the noble lords who are well known, reverenced and respected be the one to undertake this so that Your words will be believed. For it is true that I am only a poor man; I am not worthy of being there where You send me; pardon me, my Xocoyota, I do not wish to make your noble heart sad; I do not want to fall into your displeasure."

Then the always noble Virgin answered him, saying: "Hear me, my son; it is true that I do not lack for servants or ambassadors to whom I could entrust my message so that my will could be verified, but it is important that you speak for me in this matter, weary as you are; in your hands you have the means of verifying, of making plain my desire, my will; I pray you, my xocoyote, and advise you with much care, that you go again tomorrow to see the Bishop and represent me; give him an understanding of my desire, my will, that he build the church that I ask; and tell him once again that it is the eternal Virgin, Holy Mary, the Mother of God, who sends you to him."

And Juan Diego answered her, saying: "Queen of Heaven, my Holy One, my Damsel, do not trouble your heart, for I will go with all my heart and make plain Your voice, Your words. It is not because I do not want to go, or because the road is stony, but only because perhaps I would not be heard, and if I were heard I would not be believed. I will go and do your bidding and tomorrow in the afternoon about sunset I will return to give the answer to your words the Lord Bishop will make; and now I leave You, my Xocoyota, my Damsel, my Lady; meanwhile, rest You."

With this, he went to his house to rest. The next day being Sunday, he left his house in the morning and went straightway to Tlatilulco, to attend Mass and the sermon. Then, being determined to see the Bishop, when Mass and the sermon were finished, at ten o'clock, with all the other Indians he came out of the church; but Juan Diego left them and went to the palace of the Lord Bishop. And having arrived there, he spared no effort in order to see him and when, after great difficulty, he did see him again, he fell to his knees and implored him to the point of weeping, much moved, in an effort to make plain the words of the Queen of Heaven, and that the message and the will of the most resplendent Virgin would be believed; that the church be built as She asked, where She wished it.

But the Lord Bishop asked Juan Diego many things, to know for certain what had taken place, questioning him: Where did he see Her? What did the Lady look like whom he saw? And he told the Lord Bishop all that he had seen. But although he told him everything exactly, so that it seemed in all likelihood that She was the Immaculate Virgin, Mary most pure, the beloved Mother of our Lord Jesus Christ, the Bishop said he could not be certain. He said: It is not only with her words that we have to do, but also to obtain that for which she asks. It is very necessary to have some sign by which we may believe that it is really the Queen of Heaven who sends you.

And Juan Diego, having heard him, said to the Lord Bishop: "My Lord, wait for whatever sign it is that you ask for, and I will go at once to ask the Queen of Heaven, who sent me." And the Lord Bishop, seeing that he had agreed, and so that he should not be confused or worried, in any way, urged him to go; and then, calling some of his servants in whom he had much confidence, he asked them to follow and to watch where he went and see whomsoever it was that he went to see, and with whom he might speak. And this was done accordingly, and when Juan Diego reached the place where a bridge over the river, near the hill, met the royal highway, they lost him, and although they searched for him everywhere they could not find him in any part of that land. And so they returned, and not only were they weary, but extremely annoyed with him, and upon their return they abused him much with the Lord Bishop, over all that had happened, for they did not believe in him; they said that he had been deceiving him, and had imagined all that he had come to relate to him, or perhaps he had dreamed it, and they agreed and said that if he should come again they would seize him and chastise him severely so that he would not lie another time.

The next day, Monday, when Juan Diego was to bring some sign by which he might be believed, he did not return, since, when he arrived at his house, an uncle of his who was staying there, named Juan Bernardino, was very ill of a burning fever; Juan Diego went at once to bring a doctor and then he procured medicine; but there still was no time because the man was very ill. Early in the morning his uncle begged him to go out to bring one of the priests from Tlatilulco so that he might be confessed, for he was very certain that his time had come to die, now that he was too weak to rise, and could not get well.

And on Tuesday, very early in the morning, Juan Diego left his house to go to Tlatilulco to call a priest and as he was nearing the hill on the road which lies at the foot of the hill towards the west, which was his usual way, he said to himself: "If I go straight on, without doubt I will see our Lady and She will persuade me to take the sign to the Lord Bishop; let us first do our duty; I will go first to call the priest for my poor uncle; will he not be waiting for him?"

With this he turned to another road at the foot of the slope and was coming down the other side towards the east to take a short cut to Mexico; he thought that by turning that way the Queen of Heaven would not see him, but She was watching for him, and he saw Her on the hilltop where he had always seen Her before, coming down that side of the slope, by the shortest way, and She said to him:

"Xocoyote mio, where are you going? What road is this you are taking?"

And he was frightened; it is not known whether he was disgusted with himself, or was ashamed, or perhaps he was struck with wonder; he prostrated himself before Her and greeted her, saying: "My Daughter, my Xocoyota, God keep You, Lady. How did You waken? And is your most pure body well, perchance? My Holy One, I will bring pain to

your heart — for I must tell You, my Virgin, that an uncle of mine, who is
Your servant, is very sick, with an illness so strong that without doubt
he will die of it; I am hastening to Your house in Mexico to call one of
our Lord's dear ones, our priest, to come to confess him, and when I have
done that, then I will come back to carry out Your commandment. My
Virgin, my Lady, forgive me, be patient with me until I do my duty, and
then tomorrow I will come back to You."

And having heard Juan Diego's explanation, the most holy and immaculate Virgin replied to him:

"Listen, and be sure, my dear son, that I will protect you; do not be
frightened or grieve, or let your heart be dismayed; however great the
illness may be that you speak of, am I not here, I who am your mother,
and is not my help a refuge? Am I not of your kind? Do not be con-
cerned about your uncle's illness, for he is not now going to die; be
assured that he is now already well. Is there anything else needful?"
(And in that same hour his uncle was healed, as later he learned.)

And Juan Diego, having heard the words of the Queen of Heaven,
greatly rejoiced and was convinced, and besought Her that She would
send him again to see the Lord Bishop, to carry him some sign by which
he could believe, as he had asked.

Whereupon the Queen of Heaven commanded him to climb up to the
top of the hill where he had always seen her, saying: "Climb up to the top
of the hill, my xocoyote, where you have seen me stand, and there you
will find many flowers; pluck them and gather them together, and then
bring them down here to my presence."

Then Juan Diego climbed up the hill and when he had reached the top
he marvelled to see blooming there many kinds of beautiful flowers of
Castile, for it was then very cold, and he marvelled at their fragrance
and odor. Then he began to pluck them, and gathered them together
carefully, and wrapped them in his mantle, and when he had finished
he descended and carried to the Queen of Heaven all the flowers he had
plucked. She, when she had seen them, took them into her immaculate
hands, gathered them together again, and laid them in his cloak once
more and said to him:

"My xocoyote, all these flowers are the sign that you must take to the
Bishop; in my name tell him that with this he will see and recognize my
will and that he must do what I ask; and you who are my ambassador
worthy of confidence, I counsel you to take every care that you open
your mantle only in the presence of the Bishop, and you must make it
known to him what it is that you carry, and tell him how I asked you to
climb to the top of the hill to gather the flowers. Tell him also all that
you have seen, so that you will persuade the Lord Bishop and he will
see that the church is built for which I ask."

And when the Queen of Heaven had acquainted him with this, he departed, following the royal highway which leads directly to Mexico. He traveled content, because he was persuaded that now he would succeed; he walked carefully, taking great pains not to injure what he was carrying in his mantle; he went glorying in the fragrance of the beautiful flowers. When he arrived at the Bishop's palace, he encountered his majordomo and other servants and asked them to tell the Bishop that he would like to see him; but none of them would, perhaps because it was still very early in the morning or, perhaps recognizing him, they were vexed or, because they knew how others of their household had lost him on the road when they were following him. They kept him waiting there a long time; he waited very humbly to see if they would call him, and when it was getting very late, they came to him to see what it was he was carrying as a proof of what he had related. And Juan Diego, seeing that he could not hide from them what he was carrying, when they had tormented him and jostled him and knocked him about, let them glimpse that he had roses, to deliver himself from them; and they, when they saw that they were roses of Castile, very fragrant and fresh, and not at all in their season, marvelled and wanted to take some of them. Three times they made bold to take them, but they could not because, when they tried to take them, they were not roses that they touched, but were as if painted or embroidered. Upon this, they went to the Lord Bishop to tell him what they had seen, and that the Indian who was there often before had come again and wanted to see him, and that they had kept him waiting there a long time.

The Lord Bishop, having heard this, knew that now this was the sign that should persuade him whether what the Indian had told him was true. He straightway asked that he be brought in to see him.

Having come into his presence, Juan Diego fell to his knees (as he had always done) and again related fully all that he had seen, and full of satisfaction and wonder he said: "My Lord, I have done that which you asked me; I went to tell my Holy One, the Queen of Heaven, the beloved Virgin Mary, Mother of God, how you asked me for some sign that you might believe that it was She who desired you to build Her the church for which She asked. And also I told Her how I had given my word that I would bring you some sign so that you could believe in what She had put in my care, and She heard with pleasure your suggestion and found it good, and just now, early this morning, She told me to come again to see you and I asked Her for the sign that I had asked Her to give me, and then She sent me to the hilltop where I have always seen Her, to pluck the flowers that I should see there. And when I had plucked them, I took them to the foot of the mountain where She had remained, and She gathered them into her immaculate hands and then put them again into my mantle for me to bring them to you. Although I knew very well that the hilltop was not a place for flowers, since it is a place of thorns, cactuses, caves and mezquites, I was not confused and did not doubt her. When I reached the summit I saw there was a garden there of flowers with quantities of the fragrant flowers which are found in Castile; I took them and carried them to the Queen of Heaven and She told me that I must bring them to you, and now I have done it, so that you may see the sign that you ask for in order to do Her bidding, and so that you will see that my word is true. And here they are."

Whereupon he opened his white cloak, in which he was carrying the flowers, and as the roses of Castile dropped out to the floor, suddenly there appeared the most pure image of the most noble Virgin Mary, Mother of God, just exactly as it is, even now, in Her holy house, in Her church which is named Guadalupe; and the Lord Bishop, having seen this, and all those who were with him, knelt down and gazed with wonder; and then they grew sad, and were sorrowful, and were aghast, and the Lord Bishop with tenderness and weeping begged Her forgiveness for not having done Her bidding at once. And when he had finished, he untied from Juan Diego's neck the cloak on which was printed the figure of the Queen of Heaven. And then he carried it into his chapel; and Juan Diego remained all that day in the house of the Bishop, who did not want him to go. And the following day the Bishop said to him: "Come, show us where it is the Queen of Heaven wishes us to build Her church." And when he had shown them where it was, he told them that he wanted to go to his house to see his uncle Juan Bernardino who had been very ill and he had set out for Tlatilulco to get a priest to confess him, but the Queen of Heaven had told him that he was already cured.

They did not let him go alone, but went with him to his house, and when they arrived there, they saw that his uncle was well and that nothing was now the matter with him; and the uncle wondered much when he saw such a company with his nephew, and all treating him with great courtesy, and he asked him "How is it they treat you this way? And why do they reverence you so much?"

And Juan Diego told him that when he had gone from the house to call a confessor for him, he saw the Queen of Heaven on the hill called Tepeyacac and She had sent him to Mexico to see the Lord Bishop to have a church built for Her. And that She had also told him not to worry about his uncle, that he was now well.

Whereupon his uncle showed great joy and told him that it was true that at that very hour he had been healed, and that he himself had seen exactly that same Person, and that She had told him how She had sent him to Mexico to see the Bishop, and also that when he saw him again, to tell him all that he had seen also, and how, miraculously, he had been restored to health, and that the most holy Image of the Immaculate Virgin should be called Santa María de Guadalupe.

BIBLIOGRAPHY

Acta Apostolicae Sedis. Vol. XIV. Romae: Ex Typographia Vaticanis, 1895.
————. Vol. XXXV (Series II, Vol. X) Num. 7, 1943.
————. Vol. XII (Series II). Romae: Typis Polyglottis Vaticanis, 1945.
Acta Sanctae Sedis. Vol. XXXVI. Romae: Ex Typographia Polyglotta, 1903–1904.
Agüero, Victoriano (ed.). *Album de la Coronación de la Santísima Virgen de Guadalupe.* México: Imprenta del Tiempo. 1896.
Amaya, Jesús. *La Madre de Dios: Génesis e Historia de Nuestra Señora de Guadalupe.* México: Editorial Lumen, 1931.
Anonymous. *Santa María de Guadalupe: Patrona de los Mejicanos.* Guadalajara: Tip. de Ancira y Hno., 1884.
Antícoli, Esteban, S.J. *Defensa de la Aparición de la Virgen María en el Tepeyac.* Puebla, México: Imprenta del Colegio Pío de Artes y Oficios, 1893.
Bartolache, José. *Manifiesto Satisfactorio.* México: Imprenta por D. Felipe de Zúñiga, 1790.
Becerra Tanco, Luis. *La Felicidad de México.* México, 1685.
Benedict XIV. *De Servorum Dei Beatificatione et Beatorum Canonizatione.* Vol. III. Patavii: Typis Seminarii, 1743.
Beristáin de Souza, José Mariano. *Biblioteca Hispano-Americana Septentrional.* Vol. III. México: Oficina de Alejandro Valdés, 1821.
Boturini, Lorenzo. *Idea de Una Historia General de la América Septentrional.* Madrid: Imprenta de Juan Zúñiga, 1746.
Brinton, Daniel. *Ancient Nahuatl Poetry.* Philadelphia: D.C. Brinton, 1887.
Cabrera y Quintero, Cayetano. *Escudo de Armas de México.* México, 1746.
Cabrera, Miguel. *Maravilla Americana.* México: Imprenta del Real y Más Antiguo Colegio de San Ildefonso, 1756.
Carrillo y Pérez, Ignacio. *Pensil Americano, Florida en el invierno La Imagen de María Santísima de Guadalupe, etc.* México: Imprenta por D. Mariano de Zúñiga, 1797.
Clavijero, Francisco. *Historia Antigua de México y de su Conquista.* Vol. II. México: Imprenta de Lara, 1844.
Cuevas, Mariano, S.J. *Documentos Inéditos del Siglo XVI para la Historia de México.* México: Talleres del Museo Nacional de Arqueología, Historia y Etnología, 1914.

————. *Album Histórico Guadalupano del IV Centenario.* México: Basílica de Santa María de Guadalupe, 1931.

Dávila y Arrillaga, José. *Continuación de la Historia de la Compañía de Jesús en Nueva España.* Vol. I. Puebla: Imprenta del Colegio Pío de Artes y Oficios, 1888.

de la Rosa, Agustino. *Dissertatio Historico Theologica de Apparitione B.M.V. de Guadalupe.* Guadalaxarae, 1887.

Demarest, Donald and Taylor, Coley. *The Dark Virgin.* New York: Coley Taylor, Inc., 1956.

Díaz del Castillo, Bernal. *Historia Verdadera de la Conquista de la Nueva España.* Spain, 1837.

Eguiara et Eguren, Joanne Joseph. *Bibliotheca Mexicana.* Tomos Primus. Mexici, 1755.

Encíclicas Pontificales, 1832–1939. Vol. I. Buenos Aires: Editorial Guadalupe, 1958.

Fernández de Uribe, Joseph Patricio. *Disertación Histórico Crítico.* México: En la Oficina de D. Mariano de Zúñiga y Ontiveros, 1801.

————. *Sermón de Nuestra Señora de Guadalupe Predicado en su Santuario el Año 1777, Día 14 de Diciembre.* México: En la Oficina de D. Mariano Zúñiga y Ontiveros, 1801.

Florencia, Francisco de. *La Estrella del Norte de México.* México: por Doña M. de Benavides, Viuda de Juan de Rivera, En El Empedradillo, 1688.

Galindo, Enrique, M.J. *Datos Guadalupanos.* México, 1961.

Galván Rivera, Mariano (ed.). *Concilio III Provincial de México: 1585.* México: Eugenio Maillefert y Co., 1859.

García Gutiérrez, Jesús, S.J. *Efemérides Guadalupanos.* México: Antigua Imprenta de Murguia, 1931.

————. *Primer Siglo Guadalupano: Documentación Indígena y Española.* México: Imprenta Patricio Sanz, 1931.

Guridi y Alcocer, José Miguel. *Apología de la Aparición de Nuestra Señora de Guadalupe.* México: En la Oficina de Don Alejandro Valdes, 1820.

Hakluyt, Richard. *The Principal Navigations, Traffiques and Discoveries of the English Nations.* Vol. VI. New York: Dutton, 1926.

Junco, Alfonso. *Figuras y Episodios de la Historia de México: El Milagro de las Rosas.* México: Editorial Jus, 1958.

Keyes, Frances Parkinson. *The Grace of Guadalupe.* New York: Julian Messner, Inc., 1941.

Lascano, Francisco. *La Maravillosa Aparición de Santa María de Guadalupe.* México: Impreso por Rafael Cadena, 1853.

Lazo de la Vega, Luis. *Hvei Tlamahuicoltica omonexiti in ilhuicac tlatoca cihuapilli Santa María tótlaconantzin Guadalupe in nican hvei altepenahuac Mexico itocayocan Tepeyacac.* México: Imprenta de Juan Ruyz, 1649.

Lee, George, C.S. Sp. *Our Lady of Guadalupe.* New York: Catholic Publishing Co., 1946.

Lorenzana, Francisco Antonio (ed.). *Concilios Provinciales: 1ero. y 2ndo: 1555–1556.* México, 1769.

Martínez y Aguilar, Apolónio. *Teoamoztle in Nextiliztle in To Cihuatlatoca in Guadalupe: Libro de la Aparición de Nuestra Señora de Guadalupe.* San Luis Potosí, México, 1910.

Neubert, Emil, S.M. *Mary in Doctrine.* Milwaukee: The Bruce Publishing Co., 1953.

Pompa y Pompa, Antonio (ed.). *Album del IV Centenario Guadalupano.* México: Basílica de Nuestra Señora de Guadalupe, 1938.

Quinto Concilio Provincial Mexicano: 1896. México: Imprenta de El Catecismo, 1900.

Sacerdote de la Compañía de Jesús. *El Magisterio de la Iglesia y la Virgen de Guadalupe.* Querétaro, México: Imprenta de la Escuela de Artes, 1892.

Sacerdote de la Compañía de Jesús. *La Santísima Virgen de Guadalupe en México.* Vol. II. México: Tip. y Lit. La Europa, 1897.

Sahagún, Bernardo de. *Historia de las Cosas de Nueva España.* Vol. III. México: Editorial Porrua, 1956.

Sánchez, Miguel. *Imagen de la Virgen María de Dios de Guadalupe.* México: Imprenta por la Viuda de Calderón, 1648.

Santa María de Guadalupe: Patrona de los Mexicanos. Guadalajara: Tip. de Ancira y Hno., 1884.

Suárez de Peralta, Juan. *Tratado del Descubrimiento de las Indias.* Madrid Imp. de Manuel Hernández, 1878.

Summa Theologiae. Vol. I. Studii Generalis O. Pr., Ottawa, Canada, MDCCCCXLI

Tercero, Juan Luis. *La Causa Guadalupana: Los Ultimos Veinte Años.* Victoria, México: Imprenta del Gobierno del Estado, 1896.

Ternaux-Compans, H. *Voyages, Relations et Memoirs Originaux pour servir à l'histoire de la découverte de l'Amerique: Pièces sur le Mexique.* Paris 1840.

Tornel y Mendivil, Julián. *La Aparición de Nuestra Señora de Guadalupe de México.* Vol. I. Orizava [sic], México: José Ma. Naredo, 1849.

Torroella, Enrique, S.J. (ed.). *El Nican Mopohua.* México: Buena Prensa, 1961.

Velázquez, Primo Feliciano. *La Aparición de Santa María de Guadalupe.* México: Imprenta Patricio Sanz, 1931.

Vera, Fortino Hipólito. *Apuntamientos Históricos de los Concilios Provinciales Mexicanos y Privilegios de América.* México, 1893.

————. *Colección de Documentos Eclesiásticos de México.* Vol. I, Vol. II. Amecameca, México, 1887.

————. *Contestación Histórico Crítico en Defensa de la Maravillosa Aparición de la Santísima Virgen de Guadalupe.* Querétaro: Imprenta de la Escuela de Artes, 1892.

————. *Notas del Compendio Histórico del Concilio III Mexicano.* Vol. II. México: Imprenta del Colegio Católico, 1879.

————. *Información Sobre la Milagrosa Aparición de la Santísima Virgen de Guadalupe Recibida en 1666–1723.* Amecameca: Imprenta Católica, 1889.

————. *El Tesoro Guadalupano.* Amecameca, 1889.

Villanueva, Lucio, S.J. *La Inmaculada del Tepeyac.* México, 1945.

Zelaa e Hidalgo, Joseph. *Glorias de Querétaro.* México: Imprenta por D. Mariano de Zúñiga, 1803.

Manuscripts

Anales Mexicanos de Juan Bautista. Siglo XVI. Copied by Don Vicente de Paul Andrade. Biblioteca del Museo Nacional de Arqueología, Historia y Etnografía, México, Colección Gómez Orozco, MS, 14.

Carrillo y Pérez, Ignacio. Letters written in 1803 answering questions about the Cult of Our Lady of Guadalupe. Biblioteca del Museo Nacional de Arqueología, Historia y Etnografía, México, MSS, 156.

Colección de Memorias de Nueva España. Vol. I. 1790. Archivo Nacional de México.

Copy of a will given in the sixteenth century in which lands are willed to the Virgin of Guadalupe. Biblioteca del Museo Nacional de Arqueología, Historia y Etnografía, México, MSS, 156.

Document of erection of the Collegiate Church in 1750. Biblioteca del Museo Nacional de Arqueología, Historia y Etnografía, México, MS, 77.

Index to the Boturini Collection. Biblioteca del Museo Nacional de Arqueología, Historia y Etnografía, México, Collección del Museo, MS, T4-16.

Informaciones de 1666. Manuscript copy of the original. October 27, 1751. Archivos de la Basílica de Santa María de Guadalupe.

La Milagrosa Aparición de Nuestra Señora de Guadalupe. Biblioteca del Museo Nacional de Arquelogía, Historia y Etnografía, México, Colección Gómez Orozco, MS, 76.

Original Papal Bull *Suma dispositiones illius* of Benedict XIII, 1725. Archivos de la Basílica de Santa María de Guadalupe.

Original Papal Bull *Divinae gratiae munere* of Benedict XIV, July 15, 1746. Archivos de la Basílica de Santa María de Guadalupe.

Original testimony of the laying of the cornerstone of the Basilica, March 25, 1695. Archivos de la Basílica de Santa María de Guadalupe.

Report made on the founding of the "Real y Insigne Colegiata de La Santísima Virgen María Nuestra Señora de Guadalupe: Extramuros de México." Biblioteca del Museo Nacional de Arqueología, Historia y Etnografía, México, Colección Gómez Orozco, MS, 75.

Sigüenza y Góngora, Carlos de. *Primavera Indiana: Poema Sacro Histórico.* 1680, Biblioteca del Museo Nacional de Arqueología, Historia y Etnografía, México, MS, 462.

Translation of the Luis Lazo de la Vega version of the Guadalupan account. Copied by Carlos Tapia Centeno for Boturini. Biblioteca del Museo Nacional de Arqueología, Historia y Etnografía, México, MSS, 156.

Articles and Periodicals

Burrus, Ernest J. "Clavigero and the Lost Sigüenza y Góngora Manuscripts," *Estudios de Cultura Nahuatl,* I, Universidad Nacional Autónoma de México, 1959.

Carreño, Alberto María. "Nuevos documentos inéditos de don Fray Juan de Zumárraga," *Divulgación Histórica*, III, No. 2, 1941.

García Gutiérrez, Jesús, S.J. "Pío IX y la Orden Militar de Guadalupe," *Divulgación Histórica*, II, No. 3, 1940.

Garibay, Angel M. "La Maternidad Espiritual de María en el Mensaje Guadalupano," *La Maternidad Espiritual de María*. (Conferences read at the Marian Congress, Mexico City, 7–12 October 1957 and 9–12 October 1960.)

Taylor, Coley. "The Anti-Apparitionists," *Mexico Quarterly Review*, I, No. 3 (Fall 1962).

Other Sources

Basílica de Santa María de Guadalupe. Personal interviews with the Right Reverend Gregorio Aguilar y Gómez, former Acting Abbot of the Basilica of Our Lady of Guadalupe, July 1962 .

———. Personal interview with Dr. Angel M. Garibay, Canon of the Basilica of Our Lady of Guadalupe and noted Nahuatl scholar. October 1962.

———. Personal interviews with Mr. Coley Taylor, co-editor and tran"..ur of *The Dark Virgin.* July 1962; September 1962; February 1963; April 1963.

Iglesia de Nuestra Señora de los Angeles, México. Personal interview with Reverend Lucio G. Villanueva, author of *La Inmaculada del Tepeyac*, November 1962.